D1617113

Voegelin
on the
Idea of Race

Voegelin on the Idea of Race

AN ANALYSIS OF MODERN EUROPEAN RACISM

THOMAS W. HEILKE

Louisiana State University Press

Baton Rouge and London

99 98 97 96 95 94 93 92 91 90   5 4 3 2 1

Designer: Amanda McDonald Key
Typeface: Times Roman
Typesetter: G & S Typesetters, Inc.
Printer and binder: Thomson-Shore, Inc.

Library of Congress Cataloging-in-Publication Data
Heilke, Thomas W., 1960–
    Voegelin on the idea of race : an analysis of modern European
racism / Thomas W. Heilke.
        p. cm.
    Includes bibliographical references (p.).
    ISBN 0-8071-1563-0 (alk. paper)
    1. Voegelin, Eric, 1901–   Rasse und statt. 2. Voegelin, Eric,
1901–   Die rassenidee in der geistesgeschichte von Ray bis Carus.
3. Race. 4. Race relations—Europe. 5. Racism—Europe.
6. Biology—Philosophy. 7. Totalitarianism. 8. State, The.
I. Title.
GN315.H44   1990
305.8'0094—dc20   89-28160
                                                        CIP

Scripture taken from the New American Standard Bible, © 1960, 1962, 1963, 1968, 1971, 1972, 1973, 1975, 1977 by The Lockman Foundation. Used by permission.

For Natalia
a new beginning

Contents

Preface

In the twentieth century, political philosophy, including some of the very best, has in large part become an activity of commentary on other people's texts. This essay takes its humble place among the many works of that genre. I have offered here a critical exegesis of Eric Voegelin's two books on race, *Die Rassenidee in der Geistes-geschichte* and *Rasse und Staat*. My intent has been twofold. First, these books have not yet been translated, and, for historical reasons, there are few extant copies. Consequently, they remain virtually inaccessible to the English reader. The present essay represents an effort to rectify this situation by serving as an introduction to, and explication of, Voegelin's early works in light of his discussion of race and its political implications. The essay presents what I consider to be the essentials of Voegelin's thought on the problem of race and does not stray far from its central focus, Voegelin's works themselves. Consequently, it will not be of equal value for those who read German and have access to Voegelin's early works and those who do not.

Second, thoughtful people today are still trying to understand the phenomena of ideologies and their most radical political manifestations, totalitarian regimes. While this essay is a methodological analysis of race-ideas, one form of these ideas served as the ideological component of the totalitarian National Socialist regime in Germany. The essay, therefore, is also an attempt to understand a part of the totalitarian phenomenon. Voegelin's books were written over fifty years ago; equivalent problems are in evidence today, but their form and emphasis, and our insight into and knowledge of them, have expanded. I have tried to take this into account in the present exegesis. In fulfilling these two purposes, the essay also provides a background for a clearer understanding of Voegelin's mature, postwar writings, since one finds many of the themes discussed here expanded and transformed in various ways in the later works. Further, in the course of the present analysis I have extracted a series of analytical tools from Voegelin's early thought that aid in understanding political phenomena in general and the ideological claims of racism in particular.

A caveat is in order here. The two books on race do not represent "the political thought of Eric Voegelin." To make that assumption would lead to a misreading of the texts. We must consider and keep in mind Voegelin's own stated reasons for writing, and the context of his works, as the beginning and end of our own interpretation of them. In this regard, this essay is not and does not presume to be an examination of the "history of racism," nor of the "sociology of racism," nor of a myriad of other themes concerning race and racism. It is an exegesis of the currently inaccessible writings of an author on a particular topic. In keeping with my purpose, and to avoid the charges of pedantry and obscurity, I have rendered all quotations from Voegelin into English. Since his early works remain untranslated, all quotations from writings prior to 1939 are my own translations, for which I must assume full responsibility.

The essay is divided into six chapters. In the first, I examine the concepts of "primordial manner of seeing," and "archetypes," and the relationship of these two interconnected phenomena to scientific and philosophical concepts. This complex of problems is important for an understanding of politics, because men's images of themselves and the world in which they live have differed from time to time and place to place. We can also trace radical transformations in men's understanding of themselves and the world over time within one society. To avoid parochialism, a theory of politics must necessarily confront the phenomenon of differing conceptions of reality among men and come to grips with it. Voegelin's theory of archetypes represents such an attempt. It is critical for understanding modern European racism, because this form of racism presupposes an anthropology and cosmology not shared by people living prior to the seventeenth century.

The second chapter contains an elucidation of the concept of the idea, the origin of ideas, their importance in political thought and activity, and methods for studying them. Since, as I will show, race is much more a political idea than a scientific concept, we must understand what is a political idea.

The relationship of science and archetypes is reciprocal, and this relationship affects the structure and content of the ideas. Having examined the relationship from the direction of archetypes to scientific concepts and investigation in the first chapter, I analyze the inverse relationship in the third. There I discuss Voegelin's criticism of the claims of science in relation to the phenomena of life and human nature, and the effects of science on the form and content of ideas based on reality. In the fourth chapter, I outline Voegelin's account of the archetypical transformations of the phenomena of life and of human nature. This outline provides the archetypical background for understanding the intellectual and emotional persuasiveness of modern race-ideas.

In the fifth chapter, I examine two ways in which ideas are presented discursively to a community of individuals: narrative and ideology. In this chapter I display characteristics unique to race-ideas, both in the way in which such ideas are expressed and in the politics that may result from them. In the final chapter, I continue the discussion of ideology and present the logic of the race-idea as it has been unfolded in the previous five chapters. The race-idea is placed in the context of totalitarian regimes, in which it appeared in its absolute form as the fundamental political idea of a society.

There remains the most pleasurable task of thanking those who have helped this work along in various ways. Fellowships from the Alberta Heritage Scholarship Fund and from the Social Sciences and Humanities Research Council of Canada aided indirectly in preparing this book for press. A timely grant from the John M. Olin Foundation helped in the process of bringing it through press. I am grateful to the directors and very different financial contributors of all three. A thank-you to Les Thiele who in the early stages offered friendship and valuable technical assistance, and to Michael Gillespie, who in the later stages gave his encouragement and advice. I owe a great debt to Barry Cooper, who, with much patience and kindness, shepherded both me and the project with rod and staff,

as it were. I wish also to remember Thomas Goud and Kurtis Kit-
agawa, who in their own ways and in many conversations have
helped me to find the direction and meaning. My deepest gratitude,
finally, belongs to my wife, Tara Wynne, who perseveringly and en-
thusiastically supported the work from beginning to end.

Abbreviations

AG   Eric Voegelin. *Über die Form des amerikanischen Geistes.*
       Tübingen, 1928.

OH I   Eric Voegelin. *Israel and Revelation.* Baton Rouge, 1956.
       Vol. I of *Order and History.* 5 vols.

RI   Eric Voegelin. *Die Rassenidee in der Geistesgeschichte von*
       Ray bis Carus. Tübingen, 1933.

RS   Eric Voegelin. *Rasse und Staat.* Tübingen, 1933.

Voegelin
on the
Idea of Race

Introduction

> Therefore the prudent man shall keep silence in that time:
> for it is an evil time.
> —Amos of Tekoa

By his own admission, the shepherd Amos was not a prudent man, whatever else he may have been. The prophet was not silent; he spoke out against the injustice and iniquity of his time, recalling the people to the order from which they had fallen. At least in part, his message fell on deaf ears: the kings of Israel continued to "do evil in the sight of the Lord." Prophets no longer exhort us to practice justice, but men still speak up against the injustices and demonic politics of the times. One such speech, about race-ideas and ideologies, is the topic of this essay.[1]

Eric Voegelin was born in Cologne, Germany, on January 3, 1901.[2] He grew up in the Rhineland until 1910, when his family moved to Vienna. There he received his secondary and post-secondary education. He resided in Vienna until his exodus to the United States in 1938. In his teens he studied Latin, English, and Italian, obtaining private lessons in French. He also received a solid background in mathematics and the sciences, and maintained an interest in physics

1. Eric Voegelin, *Rasse und Staat* (Tübingen, 1933), and *Die Rassenidee in der Geistesgeschichte von Ray bis Carus* (Tübingen, 1933).
2. For my biographical sources I have used Ellis Sandoz, *The Voegelinian Revolution: A Biographical Introduction* (Baton Rouge, 1981); Gregor Sebba, "Prelude and Variations of the Theme of Eric Voegelin," in Ellis Sandoz (ed.), *Eric Voegelin's Thought: A Critical Appraisal* (Durham, N.C., 1982), 3–66; and Eugene Webb, *Eric Voegelin: Philosopher of History* (Seattle, 1981).

and biology in his adult years. Voegelin completed his doctorate in political science at the University of Vienna in 1922. From then until 1933, he was first a lecturer at the university, and in 1929, a year after the publication of his first book, *Über die Form des amerikanischen Geistes,* he became a *Privatdozent* in the faculty of law.

By all accounts, Voegelin's breadth of knowledge and erudition were already immense by the time he published his two books on the race-idea. Weber, Spann, Simmel, Bergson, Heidegger, and Valéry are only a few names of thinkers he had read and worked through extensively. In addition, he had studied a great deal of medieval and classical philosophy by this time, acquiring a fluent knowledge of classical Greek in the process.

The two books under examination here are a unified whole. The first, *Die Rassenidee in der Geistesgeschichte,* was published a few months after the second, *Rasse und Staat.* Publishing them at all was an act of courage for both writer and publisher. Within a year, the National Socialists in Germany had made them both "unavailable." As a consequence, they are virtually unknown. Voegelin considered *Die Rassenidee in der Geistesgeschichte* "one of [his] better efforts"; Hannah Arendt called it the "best account of race-thinking in the pattern of a history of ideas available."[3] The result of the books' publication was that Voegelin was placed on the list of those considered enemies of the Nazis; when Austria was occupied in 1938, he had to flee for his life.

Several reasons could be given for Voegelin's imprudence. Most fundamental, of course, was his desire and effort to understand, and thereby to resist, a phenomenon that had recently appeared on the European scene. The totalitarian movements, attached to their various ideologies, were quite new; the struggle to come to grips with their appearance and implications was to shape the life-work of several political theorists, including Voegelin. Within Voegelin's attempt to comprehend the new politics, there are several threads of investigation. The two most important motivations for the books—understanding and resistance—are intimately connected to one another.

In the 1930s, Voegelin spoke of "ideas." After 1943, he used

3. Hannah Arendt, *The Origins of Totalitarianism* (New York, 1973), 158.

more critically adequate terms such as "symbols of order." The distinction and development of Voegelin's terminology—an important topic in itself—can be ignored for the most part in the present essay. The significant point of contact between the early and later terminology is that body-ideas, of which race-ideas are a variety, are a constituent part of a social order. Voegelin found that this part of political science had been neglected, so that to rectify it would require a large work in itself. He was working on a complete theory of the state in the early 1930s and, when he discovered the deficiency, he began to explore the issue.[4] This deficiency combined with the political turmoil of the time were the two major factors leading to Voegelin's writing the race books. Far from being merely a reflection on the contemporary body-ideas, the two books became a critique of them.

Die Rassenidee in der Geistesgeschichte opens with the sentence: "The knowledge of man has come to grief." Race theory of the time is characterized by an "uncertainty of perspective for the essentials," and an inability of the "technical arts to grasp it in a thought-process." In consequence of this state of disarray and decay, the theoretical problem of the nature of man must be restored. The restoration must take place along the broadest possible lines, encompassing not only a discussion of man's nature, but also of the methods appropriate to securing knowledge of it. But the recovery of the methods must be preceded by a reestablishment of the problems.[5] Voegelin achieved this by reinstating the classical formulations of the questions concerning human nature in their breadth and depth.

This process of recovery was necessitated by the occlusion of the subject through the exclusion of most discourses about it. The natural sciences had arrogated to themselves the position of being the only method proper to the study of man, and of being the only method able to arrive at meaningful propositions about man. This position, and the belief that science moves in a forward line of continual progress, Voegelin called the "two basic dogmas" of the "system of natural scientific superstition" (*RI,* 9). The problems that the superstition had labeled "illusory" had to be reestablished as real and as legitimate topics of scientific investigation. This

4. Sandoz, *Voegelinian Revolution,* 60.
5. See *RI,* 1, 17, 23, and *RS,* 9–14, 16.

meant that a more adequate understanding of science had to be established. Eventually, these problems were presented in Voegelin's Walgreen Lectures under the title *The New Science of Politics*.[6]

Voegelin did not suffer fools gladly. He was critical of ideological, dogmatic, or uninformed treatment of problems: "He who makes it easy for himself in intellectual matters has no right to take part in the discussion" (*RI,* 23). Not only the race theorists, but also their opponents were objects of criticism. For the most part, Voegelin considered the opponents of the race theories to be working at a level of scientific understanding as poor as, and often poorer than, that of the race theorists themselves. Their attacks were sufficient only to anger, but not to persuade the proponents of race theories. The quality of discussion had been seriously corroded by both sides, serving only to exacerbate the problem.[7]

As a consequence of the introduction of scientistic dogmas, a lack of understanding about the questions at hand, and a poor level of debate, the argument concerning race theories had come to be interpreted as an opposition between the natural sciences and the humanities. Another purpose for writing these books, therefore, was that they should help to end this situation (*RS,* 13). The people who engage in such debates "can become the objects of inquiry, but they cannot be partners in a discussion."[8] With few exceptions, the theories of race, in a "state of decay," had become exemplars of "inauthentic thinking about man" (*RI,* 17). The segmentation of the object (man) that results from this dogmatic division between the disciplines and their concomitant methods of inquiry proves to be untenable if we consider carefully the object of inquiry. The unity of the subject and object of discussion must be reestablished. The confusion cannot be dealt with directly; it must simply be superseded and the discussion brought to a level where those who so desire may rationally engage in it. There are a number of problems with respect to the study of man and life as such, stemming from the arrogance and ignorance of some natural scientists, that Voegelin clarified in

6. Eric Voegelin, *The New Science of Politics: An Introduction* (Chicago, 1952).

7. See especially, *RS,* 12.

8. Eric Voegelin, Autobiographical Memoir (unpublished), quoted in Sandoz, *Voegelinian Revolution,* 12.

4

the course of his investigations. We will highlight them when we examine the role of the natural sciences in the race-idea.

Voegelin's two books on race can be divided into three parts. The first book, *Die Rassenidee,* is a single unit, but one that falls into two distinct sections. The first half is a study of the history of the race-idea until the beginning of the nineteenth century. The second half is a continuation of this history to the end of the nineteenth century under the theme of the "immanentization of body and person." The second book, *Rasse und Staat,* contains the other two parts. The race-idea received its initial legitimacy by claiming to be grounded in the natural sciences. The first part of the book is an examination of the systematic content of the race-ideas based on such claims, including its biological, anthropological, and ethnographical contents as a scientific theory (a theory of race). The second half of the book is a discussion of the role of the race-ideas in the creation of political communities. To take away the "novelty" of the race-idea, Voegelin introduced a discussion of body-ideas generally, of which the race-idea is one.[9] This provided both the context for the discussion of the race-idea, and a genealogy reaching back to the Greek gentilitian ideas of the state.

In sum, the books arose from the desire to restore the fundamental problematic of race-ideas and theories to its original level of articulation, and to establish the basis for a critique of the status of modern race theories. A good deal of care, precision, and knowledge was required for this. The recovery of sight is not an easy task. Voegelin wrote the books in an "evil time" in Europe; in writing them, he not only offered to restore sight for those who had lost it, he also identified the individuals responsible for this loss. The purposeful or ignorant occlusion of the whole would have reverberations in the sphere of politics, as behavior and action in that sphere are informed by the image the participants have of the nature of man.[10] Consequently, the books are seldom playful, and sometimes reveal the author's difficulty in maintaining his constraint. Matthias

---

9. See *RS,* 14, and 127ff.

10. This thesis is explicated in the first few pages of *RS,* but see also *RI,* 1–3, 7–8.

Claudias' description of another man is appropriate to the mood Voegelin presents in the two works, a mood echoed by Gregor Sebba in his reflections on those times:

> All things with and beside him proceed thither, subject to a foreign power and will; he trusts in himself and carries his life in his hands. And it is not immaterial to him, whether he go to the right or to the left.[11]

11. See Sebba, "Prelude and Variations," 10–12; Matthias Claudias, cited in Hellmut Gollwitzer, . . . *und führen, wohin du nicht willst* (Munich, 1953), 183.

6

ONE

Voegelin's Theory of Archetypes

The central topic of both of Eric Voegelin's books on race is the genesis, continuation, transformation, and effectiveness of the race-idea. This includes its underlying legitimacy, its duration in intellectual thought, and its role in the constitution of political communities. Ideas, including the race-idea, are based on an antecedent account of the subjects that engender them. These subjects are the nature of man and what Voegelin calls the "primordial phenomena" of being and existence. The accounts of the primordial phenomena, including man's own nature, are given in the form of archetypical constructions of reality as it is interpreted through the "primal manner of seeing" (*Urweise des Sehens*) (*RI*, 1–9). The present chapter is an explication and analysis of Voegelin's concepts of archetype and primal manner of seeing. I shall then have laid the foundations for an understanding of his concept of the idea (*Idee*).

In Voegelin's conception, ideas are based on the archetypical constructions determined by the primal manner of seeing. All images of man that determine the content of ideas based on human nature and experience are established by archetypes based on two essential phenomena: the phenomenon of life itself, and the nature of man. According to Voegelin, the forms that these archetypes take precede philosophical, scientific, or even mythical accounts of their subjects, the primordial phenomena.

What Voegelin meant by the primal manner of seeing may be indicated by comparison with a similar and more familiar concept developed within the narrower realm of the natural sciences, Thomas

Kuhn's concept of the paradigm.[1] Voegelin, too, discussed the emergence and transformation of archetypes largely as related to the discoveries, postulates, and methods of the natural sciences and their attendant philosophical problems. Kuhn's discourse indirectly provides a valuable commentary on parts of Voegelin's text in the form of amplification, because Kuhn's paradigms and Voegelin's archetypes have several parallel functions and share a number of similar characteristics. Kuhn's analysis does not have the philosophical depth of Voegelin's, but by beginning with the more superficial and moving to the more insightful, we may help to clarify the question.

Thomas Kuhn's basic unit of analysis is the paradigm. Margeret Masterman has divided it into three separate concepts.[2] Paradigms in their most essential sense are "metaphysical paradigms," a set of beliefs that govern perception itself. When they change, paradigms provide a new way of seeing in that they establish a new set of relational propositions that govern the interpretation of phenomena. The relationship between seeing and the paradigm is reciprocal. The paradigm itself is established as a *result* of seeing and may be superseded when it proves inadequate in explaining the phenomena and a new way of seeing creates another paradigm.[3]

Kuhn's paradigms also have a sociological quality in that they are the structure and content of received scientific opinion. They exist in a manner similar to "an accepted judicial decision in common law," but one that can be altered if "competing articulations" of the phenomena observed by the scientists prove more persuasive. In this sociological sense, according to which paradigms govern the research behavior of the scientific community, the paradigm is equivalent to the scientific regime in Michael Polanyi's "Republic of Science."[4] Scientific research and its findings (scientific truth-telling) operate within a network of traditions that in turn establish the plausibility of the research findings. In Polanyi's "Republic"

1. Thomas Kuhn, *The Structure of Scientific Revolutions* (Chicago, 1962).

2. Margeret Masterman, "The Nature of a Paradigm," in Imre Lakatos and Alan Musgrave (eds.), *Criticism and the Growth of Knowledge* (Cambridge, England, 1970), 59–89.

3. Kuhn, *Revolutions,* 120–21, and Masterman, "Paradigm," 65, 76–79.

4. Kuhn, *Revolutions,* 23, 91; Michael Polanyi, "The Republic of Science: Its Political and Economic Theory," *Minerva,* I (Autumn, 1962), 54–73.

and in Kuhn's behavioral paradigms, tensions that lead to new traditions or paradigms are brought about by anomalous findings that threaten the internal coherence of the traditions or cannot be explained within their assumptions.

Finally, paradigms can be thought to be a toolbox of instruments with which we can solve empirical problems. Problem-solving in this sense is largely an activity of explaining empirical phenomena within the confines of the paradigmatic order. The word "confines" is appropriate here, since the paradigm, if taken for granted, also provides criteria for choosing problems that "can be assumed to have solutions."[5] When they do not, the paradigm slowly and inexorably is subjected to modification, transformation, or replacement.

Kuhn's theory is incomplete in at least one major respect: he does not provide an account of the nature of scientific theory itself. Perceptions are organized and expressed, but they are not equivalent to their organization and expression. Scientific theory is the organization and expression of empirical observations, or sense-perceptions; it must be distinguished from the object of scientific study. This is important for our considerations because the object of theory and the mode of theorizing, which is language, are sometimes conflated. Such conflation produces critical difficulties in the proper understanding of a phenomenon. The distinction between theory and that which is immediately observed is important in understanding the operation of archetypes and their articulation, as we shall see further on. We will examine this problem at least briefly within the context of the natural sciences in order to make our comparison with Voegelin's concept of the archetypes complete.

Kuhn makes reference in his book to N. R. Hanson who, he said, shared his interest in some of the problems of gestalt shifts in transformations of paradigmatic ways of seeing.[6] Kuhn either misunderstood Hanson or did not consider his contribution to be of consequence, since he barely touched on the concerns that Hanson considered most important. Hanson's work is useful for filling in some of the lacunae that remain in Kuhn's treatment of the topic.

Hanson outlined a general theory of scientific discovery, of which

5. Kuhn, *Revolutions*, 37.
6. Norwood Russell Hanson, *Patterns of Discovery: An Inquiry into the Conceptual Foundations of Science* (Cambridge, Eng., 1958).

only a part interests us here, within a narrower consideration of epistemological and ontological difficulties that arise in the field of microphysics. According to Hanson, scientific theory is expressed in "language or notation."[7] If scientific theory can therefore be defined as a linguistic or notational expression of the sensory images of an observer, then sensory images and their theoretical expressions must be kept distinct unless scientific theory is to be made equivalent to its object. Consequently, if we are to give an account of scientific theories, we must do so within an understanding of language and its relationship to what it represents.

Seeing, says Hanson, is a "visual experience," producing "sense-datum pictures" that, though they are the same for everyone (who possesses the requisite sensory faculty), are variously organized by different individuals. "Seeing is not only the having of visual experiences, it is also the way in which the visual experience is had." The "optical and conceptual features of seeing" operate together, in that our sight provides the raw data of what is really there, and the articulation of what we see organizes the raw data into meaningful configurations. Pictures are neither true nor false. Statements, however, may be either true or false because they relate the components of a picture to one another; more importantly, they describe events and phenomena in terms of their "relevance" or "significance" to a larger context. The larger context, or theory, made up of a series of propositions, is knowledge. Knowledge, imparted by statements, "is not a montage of sticks, stones, colour patches and noises, but a system of propositions."

"Pictures and recordings stand for things by virtue of possessing certain properties of the original itself," whereas linguistic formulations "do not stand for things in virtue of possessing properties of the original; they do not *stand for anything*. They can state what is or could be the case." Knowledge as propositional statements is not an image of phenomena, but an assertion about the dynamic relationship of phenomena to one another. Theory based on language lets us "see that," while images only let us "see as." Theory provides the context of observation, "thread[ing] knowledge into our seeing."[8]

7. The following passage summarizes Hanson, *Patterns of Discovery*, 19–30.
8. *Ibid.*, 27, 54.

Neither Kuhn nor Hanson gave any account of the relation of the mind to reality, nor of the mechanics of perception, nor of the ontological status of the mind and the reality it perceives. As we shall see, Voegelin, too, did not consider this a matter in need of much discussion in his examination of the race-idea. It is sufficient to note that Kuhn and Hanson both implicitly accepted that the mind and physical reality have ontological status such that both are *really* there, independent of one another. Language lets us "see that," not only providing significance *to* what is really there, but *about* what is really there. Linguistic propositions reflect actual relations in the actual world that do not exist merely in the mind by habit prior to sense data. At the same time, the causal relations we "see" in nature are governed by the paradigms within which we perceive them. Thus, "causes are theory-loaded from beginning to end." Kuhn considers the problem of a "match between the ontology of a theory and its 'real' counterpart in nature . . . illusive in principle."[9] Insofar as the hypotheses derived from a paradigm can coherently explain the data, providing solutions to puzzles and making accurate predictions possible, they indicate the "truth" of the paradigm. Attempts to locate an ontological commensurability between the theoretical expression of a paradigm and the natural world these expressions represent beyond these two criteria for truth would be useless. Hanson considers an acceptable theory one that is internally coherent and able to give a comprehensive explanation of the data. When a theory fails to meet either criterion, a search for a "way of seeing" that will meet the two criteria for truth commences.

Working twenty years earlier, Voegelin made an argument similar to that of Kuhn and Hanson, but he went far beyond the limited scope of natural scientific discourse. The fundamental phenomena, the primal manner of seeing, and the archetypes engendered by the meeting of the former two are all-encompassing, whereas paradigms or ways of seeing are narrowly limited to a particular field of inquiry. The difference in scope makes the meaning of Voegelin's concepts clearer. Introducing the well-known concepts of Kuhn and of Hanson's lesser-known discussion may serve to remove the novelty of Voegelin's similar, but more fundamental, concepts.

In our brief discussion of perceptions and theorizations in the

9. *Ibid.*, 64; Kuhn, *Revolutions*, 206.

natural sciences, we have touched on five basic problems that will appear again in the context of our analysis of the archetypes: the "way of seeing" as a determinate of archetypes; the sociological and archetypical dependency of philosophical and scientific conceptualizations; the possibility of disruption and transformation of archetypes; the theoretical (philosophical and scientific) articulation of the archetypical ordering of reality; and the relationship of the mind to the phenomena of nonpsychic reality.

THE MANNER OF SEEING AND ARCHETYPES

Voegelin does not provide us with a theory of ideas. In 1933 he said he would provide one later in the context of a theory of the state-idea, but such a theory never appeared (*RS,* 121). Consequently, the early work of Voegelin lacks a completed epistemology and ontology of ideas. There is nevertheless enough information given in the earlier works and the works on race, and by some of his biographers, that we can reconstruct Voegelin's thoughts with some confidence. He did provide a basic outline of the argument. The elements of Voegelin's theory are interwoven with the various problems related directly to the race-symbols, to ideas, and to other problems in his early works. As far as possible, I have extracted the theoretical components from the narrower argument. The substance of Voegelin's discussion will be reintroduced in the second chapter.

The two basic phenomena germane to our problem, life and man's nature, are experienced as basic givens. In the third chapter we examine the difficulties that arise when scientists attempt to "explain" these basic phenomena. Suffice it to say at this point that the various possible archetypes, which are derived from the basic phenomena, are *not* attempts at "explanation," but are symbolizations of the essential elements and their relationships seen in the basic phenomena.

Derivation of the archetypes formed the first problem. Voegelin introduced the concept of the primal manner of seeing to explain the genesis of archetypes and their plurality over time. It is possible to derive numerous archetypes of the basic phenomena that appear to man. The kind of archetype established is dependent on the primal manner of seeing that establishes the images of the phenomena. The archetypical images are not historically static, but undergo transformation. At the nexus between primal vision and the genesis of any archetypical image or its transformation is the question, "how is the primary phenomenon to be understood?" (*RI,* 5). The primary phenomena we are concerned with, life and human nature, are not apprehended as monads, but consist of a manifold of characteristics that can be related and interpreted in a number of ways.

We will discuss interpretations and relations in greater detail in Chapter Two, but for the sake of clarity, even at the risk of jumping ahead, I will give an example here of what Voegelin meant. The example I have chosen is from a later work of Voegelin, *Israel and Revelation (OH* I). Besides being interesting for its own sake, it demonstrates the breadth of the archetypes and shows their power over the mind of man in his understanding of himself and his world. Finally, because of the distinct differences between the cosmological archetype of the example and our own contemporary conception of the world, the example makes clear the possibility of other archetypes.

In *Israel and Revelation,* the first volume of *Order and History,* Voegelin discussed the cosmological archetype of the order of the world that informed several societies in antiquity, including that of ancient Egypt.[10] The world was conceived of as a homogeneous cosmic whole divided into an upper and a lower level. The upper level was the realm of the stars, sun, and moon, and the dwelling-place of the gods. The lower level, the earth and its denizens, was the home of man (*OH* I, 84–85). One of the most important images within the cosmological archetype, according to Voegelin's analysis, was the image of the cycle (*OH* I, 38). The major experience leading to such an image in Egypt was the annual flooding of the Nile. Other important cycles included the daily traverse of the sun across the sky, dividing existence into regular periods of night and day, the lunar cycles of twenty-eight days between new moons, the yearly movement of the stars across the sky, and the greater twenty-eight-year lunar cycles and the precession of the equinoxes. Further, there were spatial images related to the bi-dimensional character of the Nile and its valley, which defined the boundaries of Egyptian spatial experience. These latter images also played an important role in Egyptian cosmology (*OH* I, 67).

Within the cyclical image of the universe, the upper level of the

10. *OH* I, 52–110.

sphere was thought to be the source of right order for the lower. Consequently, a point of dispensation from the former to the latter was a part of this conception. This point, which Voegelin called the "navel" of Egyptian cosmological society, was Pharaoh (*OH* I, 61). Through Pharaoh the gods dispensed divine cosmic order to the earthly realm, specifically Egyptian society, which in turn was seen as the earthly representative of cosmological order. Pharaoh was the source and representative of all justice, mercy, peace, and good order in the world. If Pharaoh failed to carry out his divinely ordained role, the entire society would suffer disorder and decay.

An Egyptian reflection on such a breakdown of the cosmological order in society is recorded in an Egyptian poem of the so-called First Intermediate Period; Voegelin entitled it "Dispute of a Man, Who Contemplates Suicide, with His Soul." [11] The First Intermediate Period was a time of turmoil. Pharaonic rule had deteriorated, and the kingdom was divided into several petty principalities. Institutional organization had broken down, resulting in hardships for the people. This was evident, for example, in a lack of organization in agriculture, which depended on centralized irrigation schemes, resulting in food shortages and famine. Social disorder and upheaval were everywhere evident. [12] Such a state of affairs could provoke a number of responses. Perhaps what remained of the government should be overthrown and a new order established. Perhaps the entire conception of cosmological order was "untrue," and the time was right for an entirely new archetypical construction of things. [13] Perhaps the gods had withdrawn themselves, or did not actually exist at all, and in either case did not matter for man's existence.

11. The complete poem, translated by John A. Wilson, can be found in James B. Pritchard (ed.), *Ancient Near Eastern Texts Relating to the Old Testament* (Princeton, 1955), 405–408.

12. A man should arouse wrath by his evil character,
    But he stirs everyone to laughter, in spite of the
        wickedness of his sin.
                                                    ("Dispute," 406)

For descriptions of the sociopolitical and economic state of affairs during this period, see Sir Alan Gardiner, *Egypt of the Pharaohs* (Oxford, 1961), 109–20, and James Henry Breasted, *A History of Egypt* (New York, 1912), 143–52.

13. An event of this kind took place when Moses led the Hebrews out of Egypt and established a historical order of society under the omnipotent, omnipresent Jahweh. That event is the principal theme of *Israel and Revelation*.

14

Voegelin suggested that, as happened in similar situations in other societies, the poet might have come to the conclusion that Pharaoh was not the exclusive representative of divine order, but that every man carried this order within his own soul, and could establish a community within the larger society on this basis (*OH* I, 61–62, 101).

None of these possibilities was realized in the decision of the man contemplating suicide. Having argued with his soul about the moral implications of committing suicide, and finding no comfort in the counterarguments of his soul, he decided to proceed with his intention. In this case, suicide was a response to the man's inability to live in a society of men who had "committed moral [and spiritual] suicide." Death was a release from the unbearable situation of a morally and spiritually sensitive person living all alone in a community of debased, corrupted men.[14] In this instance, however, suicide was not simply an escape from a difficult life. It received its moral justification in the following way: By dying, the man's soul would live in the Beyond, strengthening by its justice the divine substance, *maat*, whose mediation through the navel, Pharaoh, had broken down. Perhaps if this substance were strengthened, it would permeate society more strongly and without the mediation of Pharaoh. An individual man could not be very effective as a solitary individual here on earth in letting this ordering force permeate society, as was apparent from the political disorder. An appeal to the gods to restore society, however, would be more effective if the man moved to the Beyond than if he remained with his supplications and prayers here in this life.[15] In the Beyond, it was said, the soul may speak directly to the gods.

Numerous possibilities were open to the man, but he could not move beyond the conception of a society with Pharaoh, the mediator of the divine *maat*, at its apex. Pharaoh had to be the source and the locus of right order. The individual could not form his own community, "outside the political order immediate under God" (*OH* I,

14. To whom can I speak today?
   One's fellows are evil;
   The friends of today do not love.
                                            ("Dispute," 406)
15. This seems to be the implicit argument of Voegelin's last phrase in the middle paragraph, *OH* I, 100. See "Dispute," 407.

101).[16] Order had to be restored in society as a whole through the ordering force of the gods before human existence could take on meaning. The Egyptian remained locked within his particular archetypical conception of the relation of the gods to man and society, and man to the gods and society, and made his decision to commit suicide within this conception. In Voegelin's earlier language, the poet's primal manner of seeing was not altered by the drastic state of affairs with which he was forced to come to terms. Indeed, the radical solution of suicide reaffirmed the cosmological style of his primal manner of seeing rather than the reverse.

Historically, we know that other solutions to his questions have been possible. The historical and social circumstances of the poet governed his decision to a lesser or greater extent; he could no more have become a Marxist revolutionary than could Marxist revolutionaries have a talk with the gods. By its novelty, however, and its distance from the archetypical conceptions with which we are more familiar, the example does show us the range of possibilities of archetypical constructions of the primal phenomena. The primal phenomena we touched on here included the phenomenon of morality expressed in the soul, the discernment of the divine in the soul, the experience of social order and disorder, and the nature of man (the poet conceived of his soul as immortal and able to communicate with the gods). All of these may be seen in various ways through the primal vision, or they may not be seen at all.

With such a manifold of possibilities before us, there is an obvious quesiton: what determines how the primary phenomena are seen, and the image of them that we erect? According to Voegelin, we cannot causally explain the final image, but we can examine the necessary accompanying circumstances that allow the first primal manner of seeing, and make it persuasive for others (*RI*, 1). The two furthest poles of the explanation are embodiment (*Verleiblichung*) and fullness of time (*Reife der Zeit*) (*RI*, 1). The transformation and acceptance of the archetypes can only take place if the cultural and intellectual circumstance will allow it (I will explicate this statement presently). If transformation takes place in a historical continuum, and not through the introduction of a radically new idea upon an

16. To many Christians, for example, this would be the obvious solution.

older form of archetype,[17] the transformation may take several centuries to become complete. *Die Rassenidee in der Geistesgeschichte* is essentially a history of one such transformation.

We have said that primal vision is an essential concept in the understanding of the archetypes. This vision (*Sehen*) determines the content of the archetype from what is presented to it in the primary phenomena. These phenomena do not present themselves nakedly, but are refracted in the primal vision by the conceptual and perceptual tools available to the one who sees. Four principles are involved in this process. First, since all archetypical constructions are founded on the primary phenomena, they "cannot simply be verified; they are not simply true or false, but are also verified by the primal manner of seeing, into which they integrate themselves" (*RI*, 14). Consequently, "the primal manner of seeing and the archetypes that become visible in them can similarly not be weighed against one another in terms of their correct content—all are true, for they all see what is real" (*RI*, 14–15). There is "no argument against an archetype," because even where such arguments are found, they are intended to defend a manner of seeing, and not to defend the "correctness or falsehood of a factual assertion" (*RI*, 15), which appears only *within* a primal manner of seeing.

Second, primal ways of seeing do not impose themselves as logical necessities. There are many possibilities, given the range of the phenomena, and for any one archetype to become predominant, it must be persuasive. Persuasiveness is a matter of argument, leading to insight. Those who begin to see a new archetype must, in the face of the old one, persuade themselves and others "to let that which is seen count as real." The new manner of seeing must replace the old one; training and determination are required to overcome centuries of habit.[18]

Third, the primal vision is affected by the quality and quantity of material available to the intellect. When knowledge of a field of study or speculation expands, new possibilities are created for the

17. This would correspond to Voegelin's later symbol of the "leap in being." See especially *The World of the Polis* (Baton Rouge, 1957), 1–24, Vol. II of Voegelin, *Order and History*.

18. "It was not easy to grasp this phenomenon for the first time, and to train the eyes of others for it" (*RI*, 6).

primal vision. In this respect, Voegelin several times emphasized the importance of the eighteenth- and nineteenth-century growth of ethnographic, geographic, and historical knowledge. The new information presented by travels and historical studies provided the primary vision with new perspectives that enabled it to see new archetypes. At the foundation of any primal manner of seeing is a body of material knowledge that informs the consequent archetype. When this material knowledge expands, so do the possibilities for new archetypes.[19] If the expansion is great enough, the old archetypes may no longer be adequate for the breadth of the phenomena that engender them. A series of questions about what the new information means may bring about a transformation in the attempt adequately to answer them. The answers at the primary level are not scientific or philosophical, but archetypical. The new material engenders new manners of seeing. The primal manner of seeing is not so much a separate faculty of the psyche as a faculty of conceptualization that is a function of what it conceptualizes. This is what makes it primal.

Finally, the archetypes of human nature, even when the seeing of them rests on archetypes of the phenomenon of life, must be embodied in human individuals before they can become "effective in the minds of men" (*RI*, 15). The archetypes arise when they are embodied in persons, and they are then taken up by others as models of human existence. Voegelin includes Plato, Caesar, Jesus, and Napoleon in his list of archetypical (model) men (*RI*, 8, 15). These men "live" the archetype in a manner that can be seen by all; they are living icons who make the archetype visible and persuasive, a model for others to follow. In this respect, discipleship (*Nachfolge*) may "historically be a basic category" (*RI*, 15).

THE DEPENDENCY OF CONCEPTUALIZATION

If the archetypes of human nature must be embodied (consciously or unconsciously) by an observable human being, then the question of the "genesis of archetypes and their effectiveness in the minds of men leads to questions of a philosophy of the community and a philosophy of history" (*RI*, 15). These questions are sharpened if we consider the role of archetypes in the formation of philosophical and

---

19. See Eric Voegelin, "The Growth of the Race Idea," *Review of Politics*, II (1940), 295–99; *RI*, 6, 47–49; *RS*, 154–67.

scientific concepts. Voegelin discussed the problem in a subsection of his introduction to *Die Rassenidee in der Geistesgeschichte,* entitled *"Denkbilder und Typen"* (symbols and thought-types) (*RI,* 10–16).

Insofar as he distinguished between archetypes and symbols, Voegelin rejected the notion that philosophy was simply a "rational, conceptualizing science." "The philosopher constructs concepts and makes judgements, but they do not contain truth in the simple sense of an *adequatio rei ac intellectus*" (*RI,* 10). The concepts and judgments of the philosopher can be verified or rejected in the manner of concepts and statements specific to single scientific disciplines "through an original presenting experience" (*RI,* 10). When a new mode of seeing comes into being through the process described above, and if it gains persuasive force, the philosopher must come to grips with the new symbols (*Denkbilder*) that reveal discursively the contents of the new archetype. The intent of the new symbols is to "create a maximum of order in the world," a world "predetermined in its basic features by the directions in which archetypical people give themselves over to the possibilities of experience of the world, and further, by the fullness of individual experiences that are made in these pre-indicated directions" (*RI,* 16). The transformation of the primal manner of seeing and of the archetypes implies the transformation of philosophical symbols. The philosopher creates the "conceptual apparatus with whose help . . . the newly visible substances" of the archetype can be ordered into a philosophical system (*RI,* 10). "The philosophical symbols do not stand on their own, but function as the rational frameworks of order of a construction of the world that is structured by archetypical powers" (*RI,* 16). The transformation of the archetypes is "mirrored in the sphere of the symbols as a new ordering and grasping of basic philosophical concepts" (*RI,* 10). We will examine the reciprocal side of this relationship, that new philosophical concepts may in turn hasten the transformation of archetypes, in the third chapter.

Scientists form concepts and explore their meaning on the basis of archetypes. Accordingly, science can be neither metaphysically nor empirically neutral. Exploration and conceptualization are based on, or derived from, a "primal way of seeing." The archetypes determine the directions of natural scientific inquiry, and the content of scientific assertions. As we have seen, when scientific concepts based on an archetype are challenged, it is not necessarily the concepts, but the archetype itself that comes under attack. As with philosophical inquiry, the natural sciences may also hasten the transformation of archetypes and encourage the persuasive power of new ones.

DISRUPTION AND TRANSFORMATION

We return to our starting point, the sociology of philosophical thought and philosophy of history. The symbols of philosophical discourse and the concepts of natural scientific explanation, forming a coherent whole, cannot be divorced from the archetypes in which they are embedded. They are conditioned but not determined by history. Therefore, in order to become credible, the history of philosophical symbols must give an account of the "historical substance," the "lines of force of the archetypical contexts" on which they rest (*RI,* 16). Without this foundation, the symbols themselves are "bloodless shadows" that cannot tell us about, nor persuade us of, anything. Any philosophical speculation about the nature of man is, in the final analysis, legitimated by the context of symbols that rest on an archetype governed by the primal vision, which changes from time to time and from place to place.

In the course of our discussion thus far, we have touched on the matter of the disruption and transformation of archetypes several times. Let us draw together the threads of this discussion. We have seen that the "primal manner of seeing" is intimately connected to the transformation of the archetypes. The possibility of seeing primal phenomena in new ways is determined by the availability of factual information, by events, and by the social climate of thought that provide either the impetus or the possibility of seeing the basic phenomena in a new way. In the case of the phenomenon of man as a living being, we saw that the new archetype must be embodied by, or imputed to, a living or historical person in order to become effective as an archetype.

Concerning the matter of persuasion, we have begun to see that a reciprocal relationship exists between the modes of persuasion, philosophical and scientific argument, and the archetypes in which their theories and symbols are imbedded. The former are dependent on the latter for their symbolic and theoretical content, but at the same time, if they undertake to create rational order within the archetypical constructions, then when this ordering activity fails, the archetypes are brought into question. Here again we have come full circle to the influence of new information and events. These must be integrated into the overall order conceived on the basis of an archetypical vision. If this vision becomes rationally impossible or severely strained, the possibilities for a new manner of seeing the nature of the world arises, and with it the possibility of disruptions and transformations of the archetypes. The transformation may come from an irruption of genius, or it may be the result of an intuitive dissatisfaction with the archetype from an accumulation of information that casts doubt on the validity of the old way of seeing, or it may be the response to events that cannot be adequately dealt with under old archetypical conceptions.

At the same time, the possibilities for change can be resisted. It is possible to ascribe a number of meanings to events and new information, and some of these may be compatible or at least not incompatible with current archetypical formulations. Therefore, an essential ingredient in the process of transformation is human will, which may be motivated by curiosity, despair, dissatisfaction, a deep need for total rational order, a will to power, or any number of other human emotions. As we saw in the case of the Egyptian poet, crises and disruptions do not of necessity lead to new archetypical forms.

At this point, let us recall part of the argument begun in the first section. Kuhn and Hanson were both interested in the formation of new theories and new explanations for phenomena within the realm of the natural sciences. Kuhn explained the emergence of new theoretical and explanatory formations in terms of paradigms and crises within paradigms. The paradigmatic set of quasimetaphysical beliefs that govern perception provide a tradition within which research can be carried out and provide the conceptual and perceptual tools for such research. Paradigms are the frameworks of order within the scientific world. They form the structure and shape the process of the scientific community (Polanyi's "Republic of Science"), and give it the communal cohesion it needs to carry out its self-ordained *telos*. In Kuhn's conception, the *telos* is limited: scientists solve problems. When problems arise that can no longer be solved within the metaphysical (perceptual), structural, and dynamic dictates of the paradigm, a crisis ensues. The paradigm is deficient, so a new order of perception and activity must be found.

Hanson does not use the same analytical categories as Kuhn, thus requiring a change of focus. Hanson is interested in the problem of the same visual phenomenon presenting itself, or being interpreted, in a variety of ways. The quaint examples of a picture of birds that could be antelopes, the inkblot that is also the portrait of a man, and several other typical puzzles are enough to convince one that things are not always what they seem to be. Phenomena do not present themselves "as is," but must be interpreted into a world-view that is dynamically articulated by language. The "way of seeing" articulated linguistically is knowledge. This knowledge changes when the way of seeing can no longer explain certain phenomena adequately. A new world-view is linguistically constructed, seeing is altered, and causal connections may be linked differently. What we see in the images of phenomena has been transformed.

In comparison, Voegelin's archetypes do not have a *telos* the way that paradigms do. Their purpose, if we may use such terminology at all, is to arrange the basic phenomena presented to the mind, fashioning order in what may immediately present itself chaotically. The order is fashioned by the primal way of seeing, which emphasizes certain aspects of the phenomena or certain relationships among them. This may be done at the expense of other possibilities. Some aspects of the phenomena may not be seen at all. A contemporary example would be the loss of the experience of transcendence, which involves the exclusion of certain experiences and phenomena and an emphasis on others. Such a perspective alters a manifold of other relationships among, and interpretations of, archetypical phenomena.

Archetypes do not provide solutions or potential solutions to puzzles, but like the more limited paradigms, they do determine what are meaningful questions and answers about the basic phenomena. The questions and answers are much broader than those of paradigms or natural scientific ways of seeing, and may include questions about whether "paradigms" and "natural science" are meaningful ways of speaking at all. Like scientific paradigms, however, if archetypes can no longer serve to provide a rational order to all the known data about the world, they may be altered or discarded.

22

The way of seeing embodied in archetypical constructions is not presented only in linguistic formations. The archetypes are embodied in the behaviour and actions of great men, and in the institutions, customs, laws, etc., of societies. Music, art, architecture, and clothing, social habits and customs all serve to illustrate the predominating archetypes of a society (*AG,* 3–6). Again, Voegelin's archetypes have a much broader range than Hanson's narrower, linguistically articulated ways of seeing of the natural sciences. Knowledge in the form of language is not the only, or even the most important, consequence of the primal manner of seeing.

As we saw in the case of ancient Egypt, the order fashioned by archetypes extended across the whole of human activity. Technology, for example, is not possible without a particular conception of the world, not only in terms of its ontological status and our relationship to it, but also in terms of what we ought to do in and to the physical world. If the world is "full of gods," or even "of God," our response to problems of survival may be quite different than it would be in a society of which the predominant self-understanding is provided by the discourses of technique. Prayer and sacrifices are rational responses to problems under certain archetypical constructions. This is not just a matter of what the men of the Enlightenment called ignorance and superstitions; the responses are constituted by the primal ways of seeing that construct the archetypes within which men interpret difficulties and respond to them. Through the medium of ideas, which is discussed in the next chapter, archetypes determine the complete order of the community within which men join themselves.

ARCHETYPICAL ORDER: THEORETICAL ARTICULATION

THE PROBLEM OF CONSCIOUSNESS

We come finally to the problem of the theoretical articulation of archetypical ordering. We will consider this topic in the context of Voegelin's early discussion of the problem of consciousness. A by-product of this consideration will be that we touch on the matter of the relationship of the mind to nonpsychic reality. This will, of course, have implications for Voegelin's epistemology and ontology. I will not attempt here to "fix" Voegelin's doctrinal position on the philosophical landscape, since it is not at all clear that he had one.[20] Furthermore, he himself has reportedly admitted that he did not have an "adequate theory of consciousness" at the time he wrote the two books we are examining.[21] Consequently, his early treatment of the wider philosophical problems is not so technically precise and comprehensive as it became in his later work. Even so, if we wish to understand this material, it is wise not to venture much beyond what he wrote there; what follows is an indication of the directions in which Voegelin's thought was leading. We should also recall that Voegelin was a political scientist, and that he wrote the books in question with specific political problems in mind.

Voegelin's intellectual development up to 1943, when he began fully to formulate a theory of consciousness, was wide-ranging. Biographical accounts of his intellectual formation that emphasize one specific intellectual influence to the exclusion of others are not particularly persuasive.[22] In Voegelin's own account, numerous thinkers were important to his thought up to the time that the books on race were written.[23] Therefore, we cannot point to any single thinker and claim that he was the most important source of Voegelin's own conceptions. The influence upon Voegelin's life that is most important for an understanding of our questions here was his trip to America from 1924 to 1926 under a Laura Spelman Rockefeller Memorial Fellowship.

The sojourn resulted in Voegelin's first book, *Über die Form des amerikanischen Geistes*. In it, Voegelin provided an account of the

20. Some of Voegelin's friendly commentators have noted their inability to fix firm labels on him. See, for example, William C. Havard, Jr., "Notes on Voegelin's Contributions to Political Theory," in Sandoz (ed.), *Eric Voegelin's Thought*, 87–114: "In reading Voegelin, it does not seem possible to me to abstract a firmly fixed concept of what theory is out of the totality of the inquiries in which he is engaged. He is wary of everything that approaches a definitional fixing of the experiences he examines" (89). His unfriendly, or perhaps unthinking, commentators have stuck any number of labels on him. For examples, see Sandoz, *The Voegelinian Revolution*, 12.

21. Anibal A. Bueno, "Consciousness, Time and Transcendence in Eric Voegelin's Philosophy," in Peter J. Opitz and Gregor Sebba (eds.), *The Philosophy of Order* (Stuttgart, 1981), 95.

22. For example, see William C. Havard, Jr., "The Changing Pattern of Voegelin's Conception of History and Consciousness," *Southern Review*, VII (1971), 55.

23. Eugene Webb, *Eric Voegelin*, 21–22.

forms of philosophical and theoretical thinking he encountered during his stay in America, relating them especially to American culture as a whole. The book as such is not of great concern to the present topic, but the first two chapters contain a critical analysis of important contemporary theories of consciousness. Voegelin's intent was to contrast the kinds of philosophical questions that concerned English and continental European thinkers with those that concerned Americans. His analysis and criticisms of the theories, and his tracing of their genealogies have been adequately analyzed by Anibal Bueno.[24] We are interested here in Voegelin's first sketches of a reply to the theories he found inadequate.

Specifically, we consider Voegelin's critique of the stream-of-consciousness theories first begun and elaborated by the Europeans. The stream theory arises out of the problem of the dialectic between the "flow" of consciousness and its constituent experiential moments. Beginning with the skeptical philosophy of David Hume, and passing through Thomas Reid's transformation of Hume's skepticism, we arrive at the theoretical formulations of Franz Clemens Brentano, Shadworth H. Hodgson, and Edmund Husserl (*AG,* 19–28). The problem of the stream-of-consciousness theories in general is that if the present moment of duration in consciousness is the only certain and real existent, then "the continual existence of the self and its experiences" must somehow be explained.[25] A unity of the stream must be found, or the explication of individual existence (in consciousness) in time becomes problematic.

The treatment of this problem by the three thinkers provides the counterpoint for the first hints at Voegelin's own theory of consciousness. Bueno has analyzed Voegelin's critique of Brentano and Husserl. I will do the same for the case of Hodgson, which is similar to the other two in all aspects relevant to us. In his analysis of sense-perception, Hodgson examines the perception of a tone. The perception is called an experience; the two components of the perception, the act and the object, are called "thatness" and "whatness" respectively. In this conceptualization (*Begriffsraum*), said Voegelin, "Hodgson attempts to give several presentations of the dialectical relations of hearing" (*AG,* 56). The "whatness" of the experience is its content, and the "thatness" is the fact of its percep-

24. Bueno, "Consciousness," 92–95.
25. *Ibid.,* 93.

25

tion. The two "parts" of the experience are "distinguishable, inseparable, and commensurate," but not objects of one another. The two
"parts" are "opposite aspects" of one another and the experience;
the experience itself is nothing more than their inseparable union,
not a "third thing." [26]

Hodgson's analysis contains a "gesture of helplessness." The
terms *act* (perceiving) and *object* (content) are used as aids to
understanding (*Hilfsbegriffe*), giving a psychological quality to the
relationship between the dialectical concepts of "thatness" and
"whatness." Substituting one set of terms for the other is mislead-
ing, because there is no psychological relationship between "thatness" and "whatness." An attempt to describe the two aspects "is
exhausted in the negation that neither is the object of the other, and
that the two together are certainly not the object" (*AG*, 57–58).

The gesture did not satisfy Hodgson. He wanted to explain how
the experience of perception was possible within the dialectical
framework. He substituted "existence" and "quality" for the dialectical pair "thatness" and "whatness." Existence is the duration
of perception over a period of time, and quality is the "objective
qualification" of the perception in this period. Hodgson then had to
explain the dialectic in duration. To do so, he introduced the example of hearing tones. The sound of one tone followed by another
is not perceived as one tone, and then another tone, but the former is
held in memory, so that the perception of the first flows into the perception of the next. Through this memory, the series of tones "stands
above its elements." For example, if two tones follow closely in
time, then the experience of perception of the former can be en-
closed in the form of memory in the perception of the latter. The
perception of the two "flows together into one act"; in the perception of the second the first is driven back and becomes memory. In
the instant that the second is perceived, the first, which had a "whatness" of perception as a presentation, becomes an object in both its
aspects, becoming a representation. In the flowing psychological act
of perception, at the instant of the perception of the second tone, the
content of the first is transformed into "object." Consequently, one

26. For the excerpt from Hodgson's work, *The Metaphysic of Experience*
(4 vols.; London, 1898), I, 60, see *AG*, 57.

26

perception presents the second tone in the present and also presents "a prior part of itself together with its content" (*AG*, 58).

Hodgson returns from this example to simple perceptions, since he finds no essential difference between a simple perception and a series. "Perception as a process consists in the conversion of *content* into *object*, simply in consequence of its character as reflective process." [27] Two things follow from this. First, "the process of perceptions reflects in that it exists, and it exists in its reflection. As reflection it is a part of perception, and as existent a part of being; the one stream of consciousness is perception and existent at the same time." Second, "simple" experiences are taken as such because we cannot discern any divisions or successions in them. The actual moments of perceptions are infinitesimal and empirically and conceptually inaccessible (*AG*, 58).

Several aspects of Voegelin's criticism of Hodgson were the same as those of Brentano and Husserl. All three accounts were not just descriptions of psychological phenomena, but contained a speculative element as well. The content of the element changed, but in each case, we find a "dialecticized" concept (*AG*, 55–56, 59) that was the result of removing the concept from its original psychological meaning and transforming it into a "denatured" one. It then became possible to speak in terminologies that appeared to be "descriptive and irrefutable," but were in fact dialecticized speculative concepts no longer containing any descriptive psychological meaning.

Each speculative construction arose out of the "unsettling fact [that a] condition of consciousness has parts that have something to do with objects and acts without being objects or acts" (*AG*, 60). The problem was removed (*wegkonstruiert*) by the various constructions employed. In these cases, the philosopher did not engage in describing the phenomena that appeared to him, but erected a speculative framework around them. Voegelin was critical of the fact that the phenomena that engendered the speculation appeared to be little more than "an unsettling cause for ideal formations" (*AG*, 60). The problems that arise within the speculative systems themselves do not originate in the material, but in the systems. The material, the "stream of experiences with its components of form

27. Hodgson, *Metaphysic*, 80.

and substance," is the "primal element of the psychological acts" that engender the theories of Hodgson, Brentano, and Husserl (*AG*, 59, 65).

In summary, though the three constructions differed widely in content and symbolizations, the underlying problem was the same. Each had an element of duration in consciousness and an element that was contingent, or temporally limited. Each attempted to analyze the element of the momentary duration in the stream, and to establish a theory of perception on the basis of this analysis. In each case, the concepts that were used to symbolize both the "infinitesimal present-moment"[28] of consciousness and its duration were "dialecticized" when they were brought together in a speculative system. Therefore, the theories described nothing, but emerged as necessities from the logic of the "pseudo-psychological" concepts themselves (*AG*, 61). In Hodgson's case, the "conversion of content into object," a symbol of experience, but certainly not an explanation of anything, became the speculative element that served as the foundation of his construction.

THEORETICAL ARTICULATIONS OF ARCHETYPICAL ORDERING

Voegelin's reply to the problems of consciousness that arise in the stream of consciousness theories was that being could not be cleanly divided into a dualism of symbols on the one hand and existence on the other. All existence is filled with symbolical being, and all symbolization is filled with existential being. The two are indivisible, but a tension exists in the unity, symbolized in the dualistic Kantian expression of symbol and existence. Attempts to penetrate existence with the "attempts at formation at our disposal" squeeze out existence, leaving us only with our naked symbols, so that "the mass of existence is thinned out to a dark boundary against which we can penetrate, and that gives way elastically, but never splits so that we could glance into its Beyond" (*AG*, 20). The tensional unity of being has no resting place outside itself, and it is not a closed rational system, because "transcendence into existence is an openness that makes every conclusion to a system essentially impossible." Consequently, rational categories will not be sufficient to "grasp"

28. Bueno, "Consciousness," 93.

28

being, as it were, with absolute knowledge; the immanent tension between symbol and existence persists, and the end of the transcendent movement of consciousness remains unknown. The transcendence of consciousness into existence is a mystery. The tension between symbol and symbolized could be more adequately expressed linguistically in the category of "unity-in-duality" (*Ein-in-Zweiheit*), but this is a nonrational category that can only be understood in "patient and careful consideration of the state of affairs in its depth" (*AG,* 20).

This does not mean that we can say nothing about consciousness or about its relationship to the rest of reality. What it does mean is that such basic phenomena cannot be integrated into a closed rational-logical system. The experiences of the basic phenomena (of which consciousness is one) that serve as the constituents of archetypical constructions of reality and the symbolization of these experiences do not admit of such integration. We can say a great deal about the nature of basic phenomena, their relationship to one another, and their significance for the way we conduct ourselves in nature and within the community of men, but they cannot be penetrated to their very essence by means of rational categories. The essential nature of the basic phenomena remains a mystery.

The symbol of the "mystery" is a term essential to understanding both the early and the later Voegelin. The word is Greek, and in antiquity it had the meaning of a "secret" or "something unknown" or "hidden," but more often it seems to have referred specifically to the rites, secrets, and instruments of the mystery religions.[29] The usage that Voegelin employs is especially Pauline. A mystery is a secret belonging to God that He may reveal if He wishes, but that frequently, even when revealed, is not fully comprehensible in the understanding. It cannot be penetrated by the intellect, but must be grasped spiritually or by faith.[30] Voegelin gave the symbol the meaning of the ungraspable ground of being, and differentiated this great mystery into many smaller problems within the processes of being

29. Henry George Liddell and Robert Scott (comps.), and Henry Stuart Jones (ed.), *A Greek-English Lexicon* (Oxford, 1968), *ad loc.*

30. See 1 Cor. 15:51; Rom. 16:25, but 26b; 1 Cor. 2:6–7 and 10; Eph. 3:9 and 11–12; and especially 1 Tim. 3:9, 16.

that also remain mysteries in their essential nature. The nature of existence and the dialectic between transcendent consciousness and existence are two we have already encountered. The essences of the phenomenon of life and the nature of man are two more.[31]

Although the mysteries of being cannot be grasped, some individuals will nevertheless attempt to puncture the membrane of a particular mystery and examine the phenomena of it in the manner that one examines objects. This is accomplished through the reification of the symbols used in philosophical investigation. One example was Hodgson's dialecticization of symbols that described processes in reality. In Chapter Three we shall see how doing so can transform philosophy into ideology.

THE FREEDOM OF ARCHETYPICAL CONSTRUCTION

Voegelin gained a second important insight in America: Hodgson's kind of speculative constructions were not the only possibilities open to philosophers. He discovered that American philosophers, specifically Charles Peirce and William James, did not concern themselves with the problems of the dialectic of consciousness and its transcendent relationship to the immanent world in the manner of dialectical constructions (*AG*, 6–8, 13). The skepticism of Hume, which served as the genesis of these problems, was absent in James and Peirce.[32]

Two themes are interwoven here. The first, to which I alluded earlier, is the question of a sociology of philosophy. This topic is central to the book on the American mind. "Intellectual formations" arise out of particular communities and bear the mark of their origins. There is a relationship between the speculative forms of thinkers, their elasticity, breadth of exploration, assemblage of the data, symbols and conceptual apparatus, and the experiences these

31. Voegelin's use of the word *mystery* occurs later than the race books, but the concept itself is present from the beginning of his philosophical inquiries. "We can believe in symbolic being . . . we can doubt its existence . . . but we cannot know it." (*AG*, 20). Or, speaking of the phenomenon of life: "here we stand before a phenomenon that we must accept as unexplained" (*RI*, 10). Gregor Sebba ("Prelude and Variations," 5) first brought my attention to the symbol and Voegelin's use of it. See also Eric Voegelin, *The Ecumenic Age* (Baton Rouge, 1974), 326–35, Vol. IV of Voegelin, *Order and History*.

32. *AG*, 7, 20–25. See also 40–43, 115.

thinkers have within the formations of the communities of which they are members. Voegelin's introduction to the book and parts of the first chapter are an explication of the dynamics and motivating forces in the relationship between social and intellectual formations. The rest of the book is an examination of this relation in the lives and thought of several American thinkers. Voegelin did not use the concept of the archetype there. In its place we find intellectual formations (*geistige Gestaltungen*); the more adequate symbol, archetype, seems to have been developed later.

Two matters concerning Voegelin's insight ought to be emphasized here. First, the experiences of the philosophers are not deterministic. The conceptual formations developed by philosophers and thinkers are freely created. This freedom is not absolute, but is contained within the boundaries of the structure found in the social formation. Nevertheless, responses to these formations can and do vary widely from person to person.[33]

Second, the same basic material is available to every philosopher. The appearance of various forms of interpretation is *not* governed by the material that is itself interpreted, but by the attitude of the interpreter. We do not have an immediate perception of the basic phenomena (a later symbol for "material"), but see them only through the images we form of them.[34] The "form of the American mind" and the "form of the European mind" are, for Voegelin, "ways of seeing" that present themselves as formational unities.

This second theme is not so strongly presented in the book as the first. If the intellectual forms do not impose themselves as rigorous necessities, but if we have freedom to move within them, then it is also possible, given new intellectual formations, to transcend, reject, or synthesize them. Voegelin's study of the American mind is an example of transcending the various formations. His discovery that American thinkers got along perfectly well without the dialecticized formulations of the Europeans enabled him later to synthesize the two discourses and to resist the claims of the Europeans that such dialecticized formulations were a comprehensive unity. He

33. See *AG,* 25–26, 18.
34. "The same stream of things is the object of all philosophical discourses, but in every discourse it appears in a different picture, and we possess it only in this picture, not in its immediacy" (*AG,* 54).

no longer felt a need to restrict himself to the European form of phi-losophizing, nor to concern himself with the problems of conscious-ness in the form these discourses demanded.[35] Consequently, he could reject the dialecticized treatment of the problems of con-sciousness and regard it and the external world as a whole. In so doing, he did not simply reject the problem, but gave it a new form and focus, as we have seen.

In sum, Voegelin received a firsthand experience of the freedom of the primal vision and the possibility of rejecting archetypes. In this case, at least two possibilities of archetypical constructions of consciousness presented themselves, and Voegelin was persuaded by the internal coherence and breadth of explanation of the one in contrast to the internal contradictions and explanatory shortcomings of the other.

I have addressed here Voegelin's epistemology and ontology in-directly. Consciousness is a process (another symbol integral to Voegelin's thought) in being. The process can be symbolized and differentiated, but not conceptualized and "grasped" absolutely in rational categories and systems. Neither the ontological status of consciousness nor the existence it transcends is in doubt. The per-ception of reality is immediate, but the understanding of it, which comes through the screen of the archetypes, is not. But what is per-ceived and what is understood is real-ity. Voegelin was not an ideal-ist: existence has ontological status apart from perception or under-standing. He was not an empiricist: the truths of reality are not immediately present to the mind, nor do they impose their own meanings absolutely on the mind. We could not label him a ra-tionalist: archetypes are not "a priori," but are interpretive con-structions that arise out of the primal vision, based in and on pri-mary phenomena. The mind orders sense-perceptions, but not in an "a priori" manner. The ordering principle in the psyche imposes it-self on the phenomena, but the psyche discovered its ordering prin-ciple in the structure of the phenomena as they are presented to it in the primal manner of seeing. If we feel a pressing need to assign Voegelin a doctrinal position, at least in his earlier years, it might be

35. See Voegelin's "Autobiographical Memoir," cited in Sandoz, *Voegelinian Revolution*, 23.

something like "common-sense realism." [36] Such cataloging is in certain aspects deficient because it tends to deform part of Voegelin's thinking by compressing it into dogmatic categories. Within its limits, it is useful enough.

A NOTE ON METHODOLOGY

Through the medium of ideas, archetypes determine the form of a community in its institutions, laws, customs, traditions, and ethics. At the same time, these social formations shape the form of thought that arises from them. The genealogy of particular images and ideas can be traced to the social formations from which they arose experientially. If a particular idea or image, explicated in philosophical or scientific discourse, displays certain characteristics of form (*Formmerkmale*), then it can be traced to a particular archetype with the same characteristics. The method appears circular since an "intellectual formation" with particular characteristics belongs to an archetype with those characteristics. According to Voegelin, however, "the interpretation of the individual phenomenon cannot [be] undertaken from a preconceived schema, but must work out of the material itself, [and must] find the meaning of the material and the best method of making it visible in the material [itself]" (*AG*, 4). The method of ordering the historical material is determined by the material itself (*AG*, 13). In both *Über die Form des amerikanischen Geistes* and in the two books on European racism, Voegelin chose for the objects of his inquiry the "self-speaking phenomena" (*AG*, 6), the discursive modes, be they the articulated theories of the humanities or of the natural sciences, or the language of myths or revealed religion. His selection of materials within these modes follows the selection history itself has made. This is the only possible method available if the selection is not to be based on a "preconceived schema," such as Weber's ideal types. Reality is not to be "ordered and mastered" in rationalistic categories, but observed with a "gentle skepticism" (*AG*, 14).

"The line of meaning of history runs like a rope over an abyss

36. See William H. Halverson, *A Concise Introduction to Philosophy* (New York, 1976), 81ff. See also Sandoz, *Voegelinian Revolution*, 22, and Havard, "Changing Pattern," 55.

into which everything that cannot hold onto the rope falls" (*AG*, 14). The possibilities are endless, but only one event will take place at one time, and all events are not equal in imparting meaning to the preceding and following ones. Meaningful events are meaningful because they bestow meaning on later events that are connected to them along one or more of many strands found in the historical rope. The strands are of various thickness and length, so that the history of man "is not a continuum whose present point has accumulated the entire past in itself" (*AG*, 15). The structure of the rope is a mystery that cannot be broached with "all-encompassing definitions." The various formations found along the threads of the rope are given names, but these are only meaningful within the context of their own history.

Consequently, the histories of archetypes and ideas are only meaningful within their own contexts and on the foundations of the primary phenomena that engender them. Primary phenomena have multiple levels of meaning. Our ordering of their component parts is governed by the relations of the strata to one another and by the configurations of meaning they present to us. Therefore, when we examine what a speaker or writer means, we do so by first attempting to discover his self-interpretation of what he is doing, writing, or saying. In this way, we can determine his ordering of the basic phenomena and come to understand his conception of things, rather than imposing our conceptualization on what he has done, written, or said.

The question underlying the examination of the race-idea is "Why do societies constitute themselves one way rather than another if they all arise in the same world?" An examination of the strata and lines of symbolic meanings will give us at least part of the answer. Voegelin did not "build theories," but examined and described what he found, giving primary concern to the self-understanding of those who live in and form the structure of meaning in question.

The originators and proponents of particular ideas claim that their ideas represent coherently what is found in experience. The claim to coherence or truth is based on the criteria of "intrasystemic non-contradiction and the width and depth of archetypical vision that validates the entire system" (*RI*, 10). If they do not lay claim to rationality on the basis of these two criteria, or attribute little force to them, then rational discussion has come to an end. Barring such a dangerous circumstance, it is possible to examine ideas and symbols (or systems of symbols) on the basis of their logical coherence and their breadth of explanation. This is Voegelin's main task in the first part of *Rasse und Staat,* and it appears throughout the books in more scattered detail. The prerequisite for such an examination is some knowledge of the questions involved in the investigation of the phenomenon that has become the topic. Voegelin used especially the works of Scheler, and also the writings of Aristotle, Descartes, Kant, and the younger Fichte as his "essential sources" for an understanding of the body-soul-mind relationship. He did not "take over" their systems, but read them to gain clarity about the dimensions of the question (*RS,* 10). The body-soul-mind configuration, which lies at the heart of any discussion of race, is the beginning and ending point of any discussion on the matter. It is in examining the content of the ideas, based on archetypical constructions, that we can use the analytical tools of philosophy. These tools become less satisfactory when we discuss the basic phenomena on which the ideas are based because they may tempt us to try to transgress the limits of the mystery that is set by the very nature of the basic phenomena themselves.

TWO

Ideas and Man

PRIMARY EXPERIENCES OF HUMAN NATURE

Before we can present an analysis of Voegelin's concept of ideas, we must examine his discussion of the phenomenon of life. The reason for this seeming excursus is that the kinds of ideas important for our concerns arise from that particular phenomenon. Were we to discuss Voegelin's general conception of ideas first, we would confuse the analysis, because we would have to make anticipatory references to the problems associated with the phenomenon of life in order to make our examples relevant to the general topic. The inherent structure of the topic, namely, race ideas and race theories, forces us in this instance to follow closely the order of Voegelin's own discussion.

The phenomenon of life presents itself most immediately in our experiences of ourselves as living entities. Primary to this experience is the phenomenon of the living body. First, therefore, we must understand what is meant by "the phenomenon of the living body." Our own life and all other life-forms in our experience present themselves not only as purely physical entities, but as physical entities having vitality. The body is a physical mass formed and quickened by what can be symbolized generally as a "vital force of some kind." The duality of body and vital force just indicated is itself the phenomenon of life and may be interpreted and understood in a variety of ways. Voegelin outlined four basic kinds of human experiences that lead men to the various interpretations and understandings of their own nature. After a brief synopsis of the four categories of experiences, I will discuss Voegelin's classification of the possible theoretical constructions of the unity of the body and the vital principle. The latter is more easily understood if we outline the former.

Death is the primary experience leading to speculation about the vital principle and its relation to the material body. When the signs of vitality, variously referred to as soul, understanding, reason, or mind, are no longer present, the person is said to be dead. Only the lifeless body remains. Death leads us to distinguish between the various kinds or manners of being evidenced in a living person, because not all are present in a corpse. Therefore, human life, at least, can be conceived as a composite form of existence. The problem of the nature of the composite parts and their relationship to one another is a recurring theme in the articulation of ideas about the body (*RS,* 19). It seems that the apparent composite nature of man is the major source and focus of interpretations of the meaning of man's nature for his own individual life and his life in a community of men. The initial source of interpretation is the experience of death. Voegelin's latter three categories of human experience will show how far-reaching the experiences of composition actually are.

The second ground of speculation is the various inner faculties of man that can be ordered in a hierarchy according to the control one faculty exhibits over another. Examples would include sleep and dreaming, instinct and will, and the vital impetus and states of unconsciousness (including sleep) (*RS,* 20). Such differentiating experiences lead to questions concerning the nature of man's soul, mind, or whatever one calls that part of man made up of the faculties not directly related to the physical operations of the body. In the examples Voegelin cited, one faculty of mental activity seems to supersede or impose itself on the other. For instance, dreams indicate a fantasy, perhaps of some instinctive faculty, that can be controlled by the will, but that is given free play when the will is suppressed in sleep. To use another example, a state of unconsciousness brought about by an injury does not necessarily lead to death; the functions of the body are continued though the (rational) will does not manifest itself and appears to lie dormant. We control and direct our bodies in some ways by acts of "will," but in other respects the life-force continues its function even when the will is not active. Insofar as we begin to distinguish these inner faculties and give them names, the vital force that we originally distinguished from the material body is broken up into parts that may not even share the same ontic nature; the original duality may expand into a trinity or further.

Various experiences of power and force are a third cause of interpretive speculations. We direct actions outward from ourselves, but force can also be exerted on us from without. We can begin new things and create new things, displaying a power that begins in the mind, either in careful deliberation or apparently instantaneous inspiration, and that is manifested in the actions of our bodies. At the same time, we are also the object of actions and forces against which we find ourselves powerless. In both mind and body, we are the origins of actions, but we are also ordered into series of events over which we have no control. The very gift of life itself, our coming into being, constitutes a boundary to our will. We do not choose or even influence the choice of parents, siblings, culture, or location in the historical stream. These formative forces impose themselves upon us as incontrovertible necessities. We may respond to them in a variety of ways, and we may freely return the gift of life in suicide, but all such activity takes place within the predetermined boundaries of a given structure of being. The experiences of an effective will and the ability spontaneously to carry out its dictates, and yet of being "helplessly delivered up" (*hilflosen Ausgeliefertseins*) (*RS*, 21) to a transcendent power are the opposite poles of a dimension of human existence. Ability and inability are basic human experiences.

Finally, Voegelin points to human experiences of the other ontic classes of being as a source of differentiating constructions of man. The previous three categories of experiences were all of man experiencing himself. In this final category, man compares himself with the other ontic classes, inanimate, vegetative, and animal, and distinguishes the similarities and dissimilarities among them and between himself and them. It is possible to discover elements of each ontic class within himself, and to arrive at a compositional differentiation as a result of the discovery. The various classes are manifested as a hierarchy wherein each appears as a form in its own right, but can be combined with others, so that vegetative life combines inorganic material with the vital impetus, animal life reveals an addition of an instinctive faculty to both of these, and human life manifests all three ontic classes with the addition of the faculties of the mind. According to Voegelin, each class is independent and does not logically point up to the next, but their ontic characteristics can and do combine to form new classes in an ascending hierarchy of added characteristics.

The preceding analysis is not chronological in the sense that one type of experience and its attendant interpretations must come before another in time. Although we said that death is the initial experience that leads to a concern with the nature of man's "parts," interpretations based on this experience may be influenced by previous experiences of differentiation within man's nonmaterial nature. Thus, we may speak of more than one vital principle leaving the body in death.[1] Which aspect is chronologically first is perhaps a chicken-and-egg problem, but certain types of experiences are probably more influential than others in forming interpretations.

METHODOLOGICAL PRINCIPLES

THE NATURE OF THE SUBJECT

Thus far, I have stressed the dualism in man's experiences of himself. Dualism, however, is both a simplification and a distortion. The dualism of body and mind would not pose a difficulty if man did not in fact experience himself as a *psychophysical unity* consisting of at least two parts. A composite human being is not experienced as an accretion of parts or faculties, but as a whole that, when torn asunder, is no longer a human being. Voegelin repeatedly stressed that man's experience of himself as a unity must not be lost from view.[2] If the experience of being a unified, holistic entity and the experience of differentiated faculties and even different ontic classes of being within an individual human entity are both valid, then a number of difficulties follow. The most important of these is the problem of establishing a theoretical construction that will account for the union between the ontic parts.

It would appear from Voegelin's treatment of the sources that there has been little doubt in the minds of most investigators of the complex of problems surrounding body-ideas, that man is in fact a holistic being comprised of two or more ontic classes. In all four of Voegelin's categories of experience, which we outlined above, men's basic experiences of life itself, both within and without them-

---

1. Multiple souls and their role in death are a part of Voegelin's discussion of ancient Egyptian and Greek anthropology (*RS*, 35–36).

2. See *RI*, 28, 39, 148; *RS*, 30, 34, 64–71, 104, 108, 109, 112.

selves, point to an ontically composite nature of life. Even where attempts are made to explain the phenomenon of one part of the composite in terms of the other, the distinction between the two has already been established. For this reason alone, but also because our experience shows us the radical differences between the various ontic classes, especially between inanimate matter and the mind (or vital impetus), such reductionist epiphenomenal constructions must, in Voegelin's estimation, always fail.[3] They must fail because they deny the fundamental experience that leads to the theoretical construction in the first place, namely, that man is a unity composed of two or more natures that display inherent orders radically different from one another. It is because of our inability to experience concretely the existential link between the two or more ontic realms that the speculative problems arise at all. To make their natures parts of the same ontic phenomenon must destroy the uniqueness of one or the other of them.

In considering the nature of man, we see some elements of the theme that emerged in the discussions of Voegelin's treatment of the "stream-of-consciousness" theories reappearing. The unity of man in contradiction to the ontically distinct classes of being of which he is composed is a mystery (See *RS*, 69). Each of the classes, working together in either a duality (body-mind) or a trinity (body-mind-soul), display their own individual inherent order and together manifest themselves as a unity, a human being, at the same time.[4]

The duality of body and mind, which is the basic structural form around which Voegelin built his arguments, creates its own theoretical problems in that the mind is then equated with the animating principle that vitalizes the living body. It is important to keep this problem in mind as we examine Voegelin's four categories of constructions, because such an equivocation is difficult to sustain if we consider man's experience of other life and the unique nature of his mind in comparison to the basically instinctive character of the animating principle (soul) displayed in the behaviour of animals, and

3. See *RS*, 29, 67–69.
4. The soul in this context is taken to be a symbol for the vital principle, which, in turn, is a term for the life-function of the body, including instinctive acts of self-preservation, maintenance of the living entity, and also the inner function of all bodily organs and systems.

the purely vitalistic character of the principle of growth displayed in plants. If, with Descartes, we construe animals as mere machines, then, "we [deny] organic reality its principal and most obvious characteristic, namely, that it exhibits in each individual instance a striving of its own for existence and fulfillment, or the fact of life's willing itself." [5] If, as Bergson did, we make mind an extension of the vital principle, we have perhaps arrived at a more satisfactory solution, but we must then remain aware of the complex nature of the mind in this conception. [6] In either case, each conception of vital impetus and mind engenders its own kinds of constructions. More important for our own immediate concerns, the dualism of body and mind is not so clear as our discussion may make it seem. For the sake of simplicity, Voegelin spoke of a dualism. He was well aware, however, that this term did not give a complete account of the problem. The mind and the vital principle are not necessarily the same thing.

THE METHOD OF INVESTIGATION

Voegelin was clear about the appropriate procedures for studying the phenomenon of the psychophysical unity. [7] First, any consideration of the meaning and nature of the body and the mind, separately and in union, must begin with the basic experiences we have of them. Our experience of the body and the mind is the only *possible* basis of speculation about their nature and their apparent union. This may seem to be an obvious point, but it is obscured when we begin our own investigations, not from our own experience, but with the texts that recount the speculations of others. Therefore, in order to grasp the meaning and coherence of any philosophical or natural scientific theories, we must enucleate and elucidate the primary experiences from which they arise. This is a logical corollary to what we have already said about the relationship between natural science or philosophy and archetypes of the primal phenomena.

We must at this point recall the epistemological point that has already been considered in the context of Voegelin's discussion of

5. Hans Jonas, *The Phenomenon of Life: Toward a Philosophical Biology* (Chicago, 1966), 61. See also *RS*, 24.

6. Henri Bergson, *The Two Sources of Morality and Religion*, trans. R. Ashley Audra and Cloudesley Brereton (Garden City, N.Y., 1935).

7. What follows is a summary and interpretation of *RS*, 104–105.

consciousness. The basis of all philosophical and scientific theorizing is the experiences we have of the world and of ourselves. Any theory that contradicts the inherent order found through our experiences is accordingly invalid. For this reason, scientific or psychological theories that reduce the mind to an epiphenomenon of the body are unacceptable; they deny the natures of the two ontic realms that we experience as fundamentally unalike. At the same time, any theory that denies the experienced union of the body and the mind also must be rejected. In the words of Hans Jonas, such theories contradict "the irrepressible voice of our psychophysical experience, every one of whose acts eloquently contradicts the dualistic division."[8] We must also remember that any concepts we may develop to symbolize the ontic categories in man are "won *within* our experience of being," not *beyond* experience" (*RS,* 110). Experiences, mental, physical, and emotional, and the data about the fundamental nature of reality that they give us, must be the beginning of all theory.

Second, from the basic experiences of human nature, it is possible to derive various "dialectical forms" or "differentiated concepts" that structure thinking about the basic experiences. Differentiated concepts, according to Voegelin, are created on the basis of an "ordering of the basic experiences within the process of existence, and in the comparison of the classes of being" (*RS,* 104). As in the experiences of moment and duration in consciousness, the experiences of body and mind are experiences of moments (body and mind) held together in a unity (the human being).

Third, just as with the "stream of consciousness" theories, it is possible (and tempting) to take the dialectical concepts arising out of the body-mind experiences and to integrate them into a complete, rational system. Voegelin called such systems "speculative constructions." After identifying the "differentiated concepts," it is desirable to classify the various systems that use them according to the manner in which they conceptually unify or integrate the various experiences of human nature. Such classification is useful because it overcomes the differences in vocabulary and detail that may obscure that underlying identity of many superficially diverse constructions. Voegelin identified four basic types of constructions "in which a

8. Jonas, *Phenomenon of Life,* 61.

42

real-ontological speculation finds it necessary to fit this contradictory material of experience into a unity" (*RS*, 105). We will discuss these presently, but first we must make some prefatory remarks that both introduce and sum up Voegelin's discussion of the four types and that conclude his comments on a methodology for studying the basic nature of man.

Voegelin infrequently left anything to chance; he usually informed the reader of the most important consequences and implications of his investigations. The case of his methodological considerations just indicated is no exception: "Thus we distinguish between the classes of being as immediately experienced, the puzzles that arise out of these experiences, and their solutions" (*RS*, 105). Voegelin explained that the "only genuine task" of science is to point out experiences and the "contradictory situations of thought" to which they lead. The theme of the mystery is completed in Voegelin's conclusion that the dependence of the various classes of being on one another could not be a possible object of a science, since the nature of the relationship of the ontic classes is not the object of any experience (*RS*, 66, 69, 105). We experience the unity of the parts of our being in our unity as human beings, but the nature of the unity is an "impenetrable togetherness" (*RS*, 105). Consequently, philosophical and natural scientific systems that offer "solutions" to the problem of the togetherness transcend the proper activities of science and, by offering a spurious account, cloud the nature of the basic experiences.

Whenever Voegelin spoke of the experiences of the dialectic, whether the dialectic of moment and duration in consciousness or the dialectic of inherently diverse ontic classes or parts within a human being, he perceived in it an underlying unity.[9] The focus of the difficulty in philosophy and science was and is the impenetrability of the nature of the unity, which in each case Voegelin called a mystery of being. Voegelin appeared to resist the penetration of speech

9. *RS*, 69. In a footnote (*RS*, 108), Voegelin mentioned that for economy of space and simplicity, he would not deal with either the problem of time or the more general problem of being and becoming. Both problems are related to our topic, since they concern the nature of man as an organism, and display the same dialectical structure as the problems of consciousness or the problems of the psychophysical unity. Both problems can be subsumed under the rubric of the problem of personal identity.

in the form of theoretical conceptualization into either of these mysteries or into any similar mysteries of unity at the root of experienced reality. All speculative constructions that are attempts to solve the problem of one of these mysteries violate Voegelin's fundamental principle that such solutions are vain because they conceptualize and solve what is not in need of a solution (*RS,* 111). The mystery is not broken but obscured by such attempts at constructing systems. It may be that the creator of a construction is persuaded that by conceptualizing the various experiential parts of a dialectical unity and joining them together in his speculative construction he has solved the problem or told us something we did not already know prior to the speculation, "namely, that there are classes of being that can be presented through analysis as the unification (or division) of isolated moments" (*RS,* 108). However, he has merely attached a name to something that is experienced as a basic existential given, and about which we know no more than we did before the label was applied. While fundamental experiences do not call for solutions, they can incite us to inquire about their meaning.

There is a certain humility attached to this kind of interpretation of reality. Much can be said of the basic human experiences and their meaning for man's existence, but the order of being is constituted with boundaries that cannot be transgressed. While attempts to do so eventually will fail, they may also cause harm in that they establish the kinds of patterns of inauthentic thinking that gave rise to the modern theories of race and the destructive politics they fostered. This is not to say that our experiences of boundaries cannot be symbolized; some of Voegelin's major work consisted precisely in such symbolizations and discussions of equivalent symbolizations of other thinkers. It does mean that mysteries, even if they are given names, are nevertheless mysteries. Furthermore, Voegelin's principles of method do not imply that we cannot speak about the dialectical relationship among the various classes of being within the unified human being. Authentic theoretical thinking about this problem is distinguished from inauthentic thinking by speculations that symbolize and explicate the dialectical dynamics of experience as opposed to speculations that propose to construct definitive systems.

In light of the discussion in Chapter One, we can say that inauthentic thinking occludes the experiences that engender all speculation by reifying the symbols by which the experiences are expressed, and by integrating them into a system that claims to be an exact image of the dialectic experienced in reality. This kind of thinking breaks down, as we have seen, because the nature of the proposed unity of the dialectic, however it may be symbolized and conceptualized, is not an object of experience; only the existential fact of the unity itself constitutes such an object. Consequently, systems that explain the unity of the dialectic are not images of any reality we can possibly know experientially, but are constructions of the mind. These mental constructions are, as are all mental constructions, based on the primal manner of seeing the basic phenomena. This means that the constructions will be speculative and natural-scientific reifications of an archetype, or basic conception, of human nature.

Voegelin did not concern himself with a final, basic explanation of human nature, because he did not consider it possible to discover such an explanation. Whatever the glue that holds the human entity together may be, it cannot be found in systems of philosophical explanation. We can take this principle beyond the structural systems that conceptually bind one ontic element of man to another and apply it equally well to systems that explain man and man's activities in terms of an innate urge such as the libido, the will to power, or the activities of production. The former types of systems attempt to explain the contradictory experiences of unity and multiple ontic classes within the same entity, whereas the latter try in like manner to explain contradictory inner experiences, such as power and powerlessness, will and instinct, restraint and aggression, fate and freedom.

The preceding paragraphs have reworked and elaborated the earlier analysis of Voegelin's reply to the stream-of-consciousness theories. This repetition and elaboration serves to emphasize the importance and universality of the problems of the mysterious nature of being, to show the effect of Voegelin's epistemological principles on his method, and to introduce Voegelin's discussion of the various constructions that arise from man's basic experiences.

THE SPECULATIVE CONSTRUCTIONS OF HUMAN BEING

The four basic kinds of constructions of the unity of mind (or soul or vital principle) and body that Voegelin found in his study of philosophical discussions of the topic can be briefly summarized here.

According to Voegelin, everyone who made an attempt at speculative constructions agreed that the basic experiences (of which Voegelin established four categories) were the beginning point of the constructions. Each construction ordered and emphasized the experiences differently. Consequently, the "principles of the construction" predetermine the importance that various basic experiences will have in the attempt to construct a unity out of the diverse elements that comprise a human being.

The first construction type Voegelin called the *segmentary construction (Abschnürungskonstruktion) (RS,* 23–25). In this speculative construction a part of nature thought to be peculiar to man is segmented from the rest, and the concept of man is reduced to this special part. A human being emerges from the addition of the specifically human element (soul, reason, or mind) to a material form, the body and its faculties, that is not of itself human. Voegelin cited Descartes' dualistic conception of *res extensa* and the *res cogitans* as the classical case of this category *(RS,* 23). We have already discussed Voegelin's major criticism of this theoretical construction in connection with his treatment of human experiences: the soul as a vital principle is not unique to man, but is also seen in animals and plants. Only the mind is unique to man, but the mind and the vital principle are not simply equivalent.

The second type of construction arises immediately from the first. In the case of the segmentary construction, a human element is added to the nonhuman parts of a living being to compose a human entity. The human element may be some form of soul or of mind, and it may be localized in its connection to the nonhuman portions of the entity, or it may pervade the nonhuman portions in a manner not to be explained mechanically. The problem with this, as we have seen earlier, is that the two realms of being share in the same life-processes, and therefore cannot be so neatly divided from one another. The second type of construction, the *construction of an intermediate member,* is designed to overcome this difficulty. If the two ontic realms are to remain ontologically discrete and yet influence one another and work in harmony, the problem of their abstriction from one another can perhaps be eliminated with the introduction of a physical organ or a mental or psychic faculty that serves as a mediator between the two realms. The second construction allows us to answer the seemingly unanswerable question of the first type of construction: how does the distinctly human element engage the non-human element(s) in the entity we call man? In dividing the classifications this way, Voegelin inserted Descartes' constructions into both categories. Along with Descartes, Voegelin briefly discussed the speculations of Aristotle and Kant as examples of attempts to locate and describe an organ or a mental faculty as the intermediate member between the subhuman elements of man and his particularly human element, whatever that may be considered to be.[10] The two (or more) realms of being within man are kept separate and discrete and do not influence one another except through the speculative intermediary.

We have already considered the third type, the *hierarchical power construction,* and one of its problems, in the context of Voegelin's methodology. Man is made into a single, heterogeneous unity, so that none of the phenomena of the mental or physical realms is disregarded, but the phenomena of one realm are made "dependent variables of the phenomena of the other" (*RS,* 28). The two ontic realms are reconciled by destroying the integrity of the one and making it an epiphenomenon of the other. Voegelin discovered an epistemological difficulty with these kinds of constructions that is directly linked to their elimination of one part of the duality. If the various elements of the duality are ontically distinct from one another, it follows that different epistemological principles will apply to the recognition and study of each. Consequently, making one of the parts an epiphenomenon of the other will destroy our ability to recognize and examine it in accordance with the epistemological principles proper to it as an object (*RS,* 29). Voegelin's assumptions of ontological dissimilarity rests on our basic experiences of the two (or more) realms; if they are correct, then it follows that any attempts to erase the distinction will result in a distortion in the study of one or the other parts of human existence. The differences we experience are differences in the basic inherent order and characteristics that various physical, mental, and psychophysical faculties display. These differences can only be described as ontically distinct, since a philosophical examination of them demonstrates radically diverse ways of describing (and experiencing) them. Epi-

10. *RS,* 25–26. The intermediate members in the cases of Descartes, Aristotle, and Kant are the pituitary gland, the passive reason, and the will, respectively.

47

phenomenal constructions destroy the fundamental distinctions we employ in describing our distinct kinds of experiences. Since philosophy rests on our experiences, such constructions also eliminate the possibility of a philosophical anthropology.

Voegelin labeled his fourth and final category the *construction of the intellectual unitary form* (*RS,* 30–35). Three basic principles shape the form of this type of construction. First, in juxtaposition to the other three types, the pole of human existence from which speculation begins is the opposite one from their forms of constructions. We begin not with the experience of ontic diversity, but of existential human unity. The difference in perspective does not magically solve the problem of diversity in unity, but "merely traces a different line through the experiential complex" (*RS,* 31); the mystery of the unity remains open.

Second, the body is the "field of expression" of the soul. We cannot elaborate the implications of the phrase here; the basic outline will be sufficient for present purposes. The soul, a nonspatial, nontemporal entity, organizes inorganic matter into a body that concretely expresses the character of the soul. The soul permeates and organizes this body through the form of an "inner" or "pneumatic" body (*RS,* 32) that is the seat of instinctive and bodily functions directed by the formative soul. Voegelin described the unity of the pneumatically permeated body in terms of three dualistic oppositions: mechanical and dynamic space; time and duration; outer body and inner, or pneumatic, body. An animal organism, in all its function and behavior, including self-preservation, reproduction, and recovery from injuries, is the "outwardly realized image of the psychical characteristics of the animal" (*RS,* 32). The postulation of a "pneumatic body" through which the soul permeates the physical body was engendered by the realization that the psychical function could not be localized in the manner indicated by a construction of an intermediate member.

Third, analogous to the animal body, "human existence in the totality of its functions is understood to be the field of expression of the personal mind" (*RS,* 32). The human mind is not an addition to the animal entity, but a primary substance, "like the animal soul." Consequently, the "physical and psychical functions of a man are the complete expression of the effective mind" (*RS,* 32). The mind

48

static characteristics that inhere in the phenomena as they are displayed to us through the framework of the primal manner of seeing. Seen from the side of the phenomena of reality, ideas are a constituent part of their being, being manifested in the form that matter and nonmaterial phenomena, animate or inanimate, assume, and in the manifold relationships that these phenomena have to one another.

The preceding account would indicate that, in the words of Bertrand Russell, ideas have a "very peculiar kind of being."[14] Because of the many meanings that have accrued to the word "idea" in the English language, it might be beneficial, as Russell did, to substitute the word "universal" for "idea" here.[15] Keeping this in mind, we see more easily the sense in saying that ideas (universals) do not *exist* (come into being and pass out of being), but "subsist" or "have being."[16] Ideas do not depend on existent things for themselves "to be." However, according to Voegelin, we can only have knowledge of ideas through our experiences of existing things. This is also why, despite ideas having a "peculiar kind of being," we continue to predicate of them existentially. Existential descriptions of our experience of ideas are necessary because *we* are existing beings, because *we* use existential language. Our descriptions of ideas, using terms such as "structure," "content," and "element," therefore remain metaphorical. This is also the case when we treat ideas as if they were themselves objects.

Ideas, therefore, constitute a boundary to language and experience. The formation of some kind of proto-matter (the oneness without form or differentiation) by ideas (through which we distinguish unique entities and also see their unity) in a realm of pre-existence (*Vorsein*) is not a description of experience, nor the possible object of any experience. Proto-matter and idea in this sense are "analytically removed moments"[17] that express the experience of a "twinning (*Gezweiung*) on the levels of being" (*RS*, 109). To take the two analytical concepts of proto-matter and idea and make them into "independent entities" that actually exist in a pre-

14. Bertrand Russell, *The Problems of Philosophy* (Oxford, 1912), 56.
15. *Ibid.*, 19–24, 53.
16. *Ibid.*, 57.
17. The "analytical removal" is the "intellectual activity" that conceptually detaches the idea from matter. This mental activity is the *only* way in which one can grasp ideas in a manner appropriate to their "peculiar kind of being."

existential realm is to hypostatize the concepts, and so is an attempt to rupture the boundary of the experiences they symbolize.[18]

Thus far, our outline of Voegelin's conception of ideas has shown it to be close to one interpretation of Plato's.[19] The only real novelty in this part of Voegelin's presentation, short as it was, was the explication of the role of experience in our knowledge of ideas. When we introduced to this explication the previous theme of mystery, the boundary of experience and speech symbolized by idea also became visible.

MIND AND IDEA

Voegelin's more penetrating insight was that ideas could be used as political tools and political weapons. How this is possible becomes apparent when we consider one of the three lateral points of the structure of ideas, the archetype, more carefully. We said earlier that ideas are based on an antecedent account of the subject that engenders them. As we know from Voegelin's discussion, the antecedent account is rendered by the archetypical description and understanding of reality that has persuasive force in a given community of men. Voegelin also implied that "things have a stable nature of their own that does not depend on our perception of them."[20] At the same time, "our perception of them" is not absolute, and since by their very nature they may be viewed from more than one perspective, they may also admit of more than one interpretation, and we may come to understand the nature of the phenomena of reality in a variety of ways. That much is review.

18. *RS*, 109. The concept of hypostasis (which Voegelin borrowed from Plato) signifies the process of reifying analytical concepts that are, by the act of reification, considered to have independent existence. The term itself generally occurs in the post-war writings of Voegelin, but it appears to my knowledge for the first time in *RS*.

19. G. M. A. Grube, in *Plato's Thought* (Boston, 1958), for example, treats Plato's ideas as reified entities that exist in a realm of their own, and are perhaps mystically accessible to the human mind. (See 26, 35, 49.) Randall, in *Plato: Dramatist*, doubts that Plato had a doctrine of knowledge at all (198), and further doubts that ideas have any ontological status apart from human speech (196–97). According to Randall, ideas are mythical formations, not "literal fact" (193). Bertrand Russell (*Problems of Philosophy*), and Stanley Rosen ("Ideas") fall between these two extremes. Rosen's interpretation of Plato seems to come closest to Voegelin's conception of ideas as we have traced it thus far.

20. Grube, *Plato's Thought*, 13. See also Plato, *Cratylus*, 386d–e.

If ideas, insofar as we have knowledge of them, are bound to phenomena but are at the same time eternal in the sense that they are nonexistent, subsisting beyond existence, then how can we say that the content of an idea is a function of the archetypical understanding of the people who have the particular idea? It is possible to do so only if the given structure of reality is such that a multitude of ideas inhere in any phenomenon, so that our perception of the idea(s) is dependent on the perspective we assume toward the primordial phenomena through a primal manner of seeing. We know that several ideas inhere in a particular phenomenon on the basis of our discovery of the manifold of experiences we can have of reality and the variety of ways in which these experiences can be interpreted.

Ideas are the "real substance" of the "oneness" that is seen in a manifold of exemplars. Voegelian spoke of ideas as entities that are "seen" in accordance with "the structure of the speculative field" (*RS,* 117). If we conceive of a phenomenon "to be" something, the "something" that we say "it is" is the idea we have of it. To use one of Voegelin's examples, the "idea of man" can be "seen" as mind, or we can "grasp" the idea of man as his animal soul, or the idea of man can be "set" in the unified entity that is man (*RS,* 117). Each predicate we employ to symbolize man's essential "man-ness" is an idea of man. The particular idea we have of man is the central predicate of human beings that we use to distinguish them from all other forms of life. In general, then, the essential qualities we predicate of an experiential phenomenon are the idea(s) we have of it.

It is in the reciprocal relationship between subsisting idea and the seeing or having mind that we encounter the subjective and objective poles of the idea. The objective pole has been covered in what we have said about the relationship of the idea to matter. The subjective pole of the idea is found in the relationship between the idea and mind, apart from the phenomenon in which the idea is seen. This does *not* mean that the idea *exists* in a realm of its own, but that the idea as it is experienced must be real in the *minds* of those who have it; those people then manifest the idea in their actions, speech, and behavior with respect to the phenomena of which they have the ideas. The subjective pole of the idea is experienced and expressed most strongly in the phenomenon of a community of men. For this reason, Voegelin's entire analysis of the subjective pole takes places within a political context. Insofar as ideas are subjective, they are *expressed*. Expressions, whether in the form of myth, philosophy, revelation, or some other symbolic form, generally take place within a group of men, so that it makes sense to speak of the subjective nature of the idea within the context of a community.

The human mind is the "point of transition" of "the idea as historically real" (*RS*, 120). In its ability to reason, to think discursively, and in its "self-awareness" as an "active center" (*Aktzentrum*), the human mind can both "see" the unity (the idea) of the manifold and, in a reflective process, use the ideas it sees to create "intellectual worlds" that in turn are manifested in the activities of the men who see them. According to Voegelin, ideas are manifested in "customs and laws, mythical consciousness, and the technical practice of daily life with its rules and prohibitions, etc." (*RS*, 120). All these intellectual formations and physical practices within a community and in individual life are manifestations of an idea. Further, these manifestations make the ideas they express accessible to an observer, so that the idea retains both poles of its analytical structure. Therefore, we both have and express ideas. "The individual mind is the locus of irruption of the idea as it is objectively understood and at the same time a locus of development of the idea as it is subjectively intended. The idea *is* not merely in the manner of an object, it also *becomes* in the minds of those who have it" (*RS*, 120). Politically, ideas are manifested in the reality of an actual community, and also display an effectiveness in the maintenance of the community. In Voegelin's conception, the community is in a continual process of becoming; it is renewed through the continual creation of intellectual formations and the reworking of ideas of the community in the minds of its members. Insofar as mental or intellectual formations are an integral part of the structure of a community, it would appear that "national types are not illusions, but objects of experience" (*RS*, 120). In sum, "the individual mind of a person is the locus at which an idea is grasped as objectively subsisting and at the same time is developed, that is, becomes actual in this act of grasping" (*RS*, 121).

We noted earlier that Voegelin did not provide a complete theory of ideas, but intended to do so later. The most important gap in his theory was an explanation of the exact nature of the relationship between the mind and ideas. Even if this relationship could not, in the final analysis, be explained, there is no doubt that a thorough presentation of the problems would have been helpful. As it is, we are left with Voegelin's summary remark that it is sufficient for the purposes of his analysis to "recognize the individual mind as the point of contact of objective and subjective ideas, and to know what idea means when we speak of its role for the establishment of a community" (*RS*, 121).

Voegelin's most important early political insight is provided in his introduction to *Rasse und Staat;* in his later work, *Der Autoritäre Staat,* he elaborated upon it.[21] The insight—a reaffirmation of pre-positivist political theory—was that a state or a community consists of more than the people in it and more than the positive rules that govern their behavior. Men do not merely behave, but also act, and they impute meaning to both their behavior and actions. A community is not made up merely of atomistic bundles of self-directed movement, but consists in a complex web of relationships and hierarchies of power and authority. Meaning is imputed to all these constituent elements. In large part, meaning comes from a comparison between the ideas a community expresses in all its aspects, and the ideas its members have of reality in general. In other words, the order displayed by a community of men conforms, to a considerable extent, to the order that its members find in the rest of the reality. The relationship of the community and its members to the rest of reality provides it and its members with the context of meaning. The order is transmitted and understood through the medium of symbols that are engendered by ideas, which then become effective intellectual tools in establishing a communal order.[22] Insofar as ideas are based on experience, they cannot be judged in terms of their rightness or wrongness.[23] On the level of expression (whether the expres-

21. Eric Voegelin, *Der Autoritäre Staat* (Vienna, 1936).
22. Voegelin's resistance to a positivistic analysis of political communities was directed largely at Hans Kelsen, one of his teachers and a leading proponent of the school of legal positivism. See *RS*, 2–7, and *Autoritäre Staat,* 102–11. Voegelin's discussion of Kelsen's theory of the state extends to p. 150. For a consideration of ideas as tools, see *RI,* 160.
23. *RS,* 118. See Voegelin, "Growth of the Race Idea," 284. Voegelin later used the symbols of openness and closure to indicate the two kinds of experiential attitudes that shape the possibilities of experiencing reality or revolting against its structure. The symbolization of experience and the ideas arising out of experience

sion is in the form of myth, philosophical discourse, or revelation), our ideas are articulated by political symbols, which can become weapons employed against those who have other ideas that may be based on other archetypes of reality. Ideas can also become tools insofar as they construct the intellectual framework that is the core of a community of men.

It is doubtful that there are any ideas about any phenomenon that could not contribute to an understanding of reality that would then influence ideas of the community. However, Voegelin insisted that "the roots of the state must be sought in the nature of man" (*RS*, 2). Consequently, the most important ideas with respect to the self-interpretations and constitution of communities will be ideas based on the nature of man and man's place in the order of things. It is doubtless a truism to add that ideas we have of man are likely to be shaped by ideas we have of nonhuman phenomena, and that ideas we have of the latter will also be shaped by our ideas of the former, in a reciprocal relationship.[24]

By now it should be clear that ideas *in a political sense* do not represent an "attempt to describe reality as it is" but "[set] up symbols . . . which have the function of creating the image of a group as a unit." Political ideas are symbolic; they are neither theories nor "instruments of cognition."[25] The symbols that arise out of an idea are the "emotional and volitional" forces that weld together a group of people into a communal unity. Although ideas do not *conceptually* or analytically describe empirical reality, they are based on reality in that they arise out of particular experiences. The political symbolization of the basic experiences taken to be central to the meaning of man's existence is the source of the persuasive and constructive power of ideas. Symbolization is grounded in reality; it is an expression of an idea.

---

would be primarly functions of the degree of openness or closure an individual demonstrated toward the manifold phenomena of reality. (See Voegelin, *Science, Politics, and Gnosticism* [Chicago, 1968], 18, 22, 36–37, etc.) Voegelin was aware that there were "ethical and metaphysical" differences in value between ideas, but criticism could not occur on the level of ideas, because it would amount to no more than a dogmatic struggle; criticism or resistance must occur with respect to the attitude toward experiential reality.

24. See, for example, Jonas, *Phenomenon of Life*, 33–37.
25. Voegelin, "Growth of the Race Idea," 284.

Because political symbols are an expression of the real substance of the oneness we see in the individual occurrences of phenomena, rather than the real substance itself, as Voegelin said ideas actually were, symbol and idea are not equivalent, nor are political ideas and ideas per se. Political ideas carry an element of intent; based on real experience, they are used as tools to make things, namely communities. Symbols are engendered by political ideas, and are compact articulations of complexes of meaning around which communities of men constitute themselves in their entirety. Political ideas may also be called symbolic ideas. If political symbols are not intended empirically to describe social or any other kind of reality, but to constitute it, they cannot be defined. As indices of meaning, not of empirical reality, they are objects of inquiry as constituent parts of political reality; they are not theoretical concepts, nor can they be used as such.[26]

Voegelin's vocabulary was ambiguous or unclear on this matter. If we want to preserve the notion of the idea as a universal, we shall have to interpret Voegelin to mean that political symbols inhere in reality insofar as they represent ideas of social reality, rather than what he called "empirical reality." The element of intent in political ideas stems from their subjective pole. In ideas of "empirical reality" this subjective pole is suppressed, becoming an outgrowth of the primal manner of seeing. Thus, there is a reciprocal relationship between the objective and subjective poles of the political idea; a community of men is in a constant state of becoming at the same time that it concretely exists (*RS,* 120). The political idea, grounded in the reality of human experience, represents through political symbols the experienced order of the community to the minds of its members at the same time that it fashions that order in their minds.

BODY-IDEAS

Man is a composite being. If we order a community in conformity with an idea of the essence of man, it is possible to do so on the basis of a multitude of ideas; we may establish a community on the basis of any idea we take to be the essence of man. Voegelin divided all ideas of man into two discrete categories: those based on man's unitary being, and those based on a segment of the whole.

26. See Voegelin, *Autoritäre Staat,* 8, and *The New Science,* 30.

Ideas of man that consider man's essence his reason, his transcendent soul, his mind, etc., fall into the latter category, whereas ideas of man as a unitary being, even where one part of the entity is dependent on, but not an epiphenomenon of the other(s), fall into the former category. Neither category of ideas could be judged to be right or wrong. Voegelin insisted that, analytically, the two categories were irreconcilable (*RS*, 118); man could not be seen in terms of both categories at once.

Ideas about man in both categories could be arranged in a hierarchical order, beginning with an idea of mankind, which could then be narrowed to the idea of a specific community, which could in turn be separated into ideas of the individual. The idea of humanity or mankind gives all other ideas of man their unity, but any idea in any rank of the hierarchy (there are intermediate steps in the threefold scheme) can be taken up as the central motif of the meaning of existence for an individual or a community. "The individual person," said Voegelin, "can lead his conscious life on any of the stata of ideas." [27] By implication he can live within either the unitary or the segmentary categories of ideas of man.

Apart from the account given by a philosophical anthropology, which is based on an archetype of man, the content of an idea of man is determined by the location of the idea in the hierarchy of ideas, whether the idea is based on a segmentary or unitary conception of man, and by "the particular part" that is taken as central to an idea of man, and is "considered essential for the construction of the community" (*RS*, 121). In the case of segmentary constructions, the account that a philosophical anthropology will give of the nature of man determines the part of man that is seen as his essence (*RS*, 121). Segmentary ideas of man within a community are not mutually exclusive. Several ideas may be meshed together to form a complex of meaning. Ideas based on man's physical, psychical, and mental nature may be combined to form a meaningful context within which individuals, families, groups, and entire communities understand themselves.

One of the parts of man that may serve as a source of political ideas is his body. We have already spoken of some of man's experiences in

27. *RS*, 119. Historical examples of the various strata are given in *RS*, 119.

the body, including death, power and powerlessness, and fate, *i.e.,* the experience of being woven into a biological series of individuals or of being restrained by the limitations of the body, which may be different from the limitations others appear to experience. From these and other experiences we can derive a category of ideas called body-ideas. Body-ideas are important in general, because "body experiences are basic human experiences and every symbol which can use them as a material starting point can be sure of a strong emotional hold over its believers." Body-ideas were important for Voegelin's considerations in relation to race-ideas, because the latter are a subcategory of the former.[28] For the most part, he restricted himself to those aspects of body-ideas that were of concern for the narrower topic.

Under these terms, Voegelin described three possible types of body-ideas that could include race-ideas. The first is a segmentary idea. In terms of his body, man is seen to belong to the animal kingdom, being the member of a species, *Homo sapiens,* and perhaps of a subspecies, which could be called a race. The emphasis in this idea is on the objective pole, since the physical part of man's nature, insofar as it partakes of species and race, does not influence the intellectual sphere. In this body-idea, there is "as such . . . nothing specifically human—the same considerations would be valid for any animal species" (*RS,* 123).

The second body-idea also belongs to the segmentary category. Man is still objectively an animalistic entity, but this part of his nature affects his possibilities in the realm of the mind. Man's mind is bound to his body, so that the body's place is seen as a fate with which the individual mind must come to terms. "Coming to terms" may mean that the individual struggles against the sensual restraints of the body on the mind. Such an idea may inform the entire order

28. Voegelin, "Growth of the Race Idea," 316, 286. I have translated *Leibidee* and *Rassenidee* as "body-idea" and "race-idea" respectively. The hyphenated word captures more exactly the sense of the German than "ideas of the body" or "ideas of race." Political ideas in this sense are not *of* anything per se, but are *based* on a phenomenon that then becomes a source of meaning for life. Although the English genetive may carry the required sense of an object, that is, the sense that ideas reside in and arise from the phenomena of the body, this sense is better conveyed by the otherwise inelegant use of a hyphen. Voegelin did not use a hyphen in "The Growth of the Race Idea."

of a community, including its laws, customs, and institutions. In another conception of physical determination, "coming to terms" means that the individual must accept his "lot in life" as it has been determined by his birth into a certain community, or echelon of that community. Under this idea of physical determination, the original, objective idea of biological series has been transformed into one or more of the subjective ideas of dynasty, clanship, bloodlines, etc. Imbedded in these subjective ideas are further ideas of inheritance rights, matriarchical or patriarchical descent, and so on.

Finally, we may also derive body-ideas from the unitary idea of man as a body permeated by the mind. The distinction between this third category of body-ideas and the previous one appeared to be purely analytical, since Voegelin noted that the two categories always appear in tandem in any historical instance of one or the other. Thus, "we find the idea of the unitary being everywhere where, from the idea of the community, the connection of the mind is understood as penetrating down to the body as its carrier" (*RS*, 125). Consequently, the unitary idea is not restricted to modern theories of race, but is found even in some cultic ideas of antiquity. As an example, Voegelin noted the cultic ancestor-worship of the Greeks, in which the relationship of the members of the cult is symbolized in their common descent from an ancestor. The idea of a common ancestor is unitary insofar as it also implies that certain mental or spiritual traits are passed on by the ancestor and shared by his descendants.

All three of these particular body-ideas can be transformed into race-ideas. In the case of the first, race is essentially irrelevant for the freedom of the mind and the freedom to act. Race is the idea of the relatedness of a group of individuals based on certain notions of biological descent and common (inherited) physical characteristics among members of the group. This idea of race can be transferred in whole to the second and third categories of body-idea, where the political consequences of race-thinking become clearer.

The second category of body-ideas expands the possibilities of the race-idea, so that one's race may affect the life of the mind in a number of ways. A race-idea may include one in certain groups with specific social and political privileges and restrictions, and exclude one from other groups and their attendant sociopolitical freedoms and limitations. For example, with the introduction of the idea of ruling and subject races within a community, individuals are locked into specific groups with their respective privileges and disadvantages. The idea of race may also be used to differentiate one's community from others, with the attendant inferences of superiority and inferiority. In each case, the fate experienced in the physical body is not directly transferred into the psychological realm, in the sense that the quality of the individual mind or its formations is *directly* dependent on its connection to a particular (racial) body, but one's racial fate will determine the parameters within which one may act and some of the external factors that may be important for the life of the mind.

The third type of body-ideas, when used in the formation of race-ideas, will join mind and body so that the mind and its creations (all intellectual and cultural formations of a given community) are determined, in general, by one's membership in a race. I say in general, since it appears that even under this idea, race is not thought to determine completely the workings of the mind, but to establish the limits of the possibilities. By virtue of racial descent, certain mental characteristics, abilities, and predispositions are determined in such a way that the freedom of the mind is limited, and channeled in certain directions.

Being a subcategory of body-ideas, race-ideas also have a hierarchical form, so that they can be stretched out on Voegelin's frame of the three-part hierarchy of mankind, community, and individual, with its manifold intermediate steps. As with general body-ideas, any point in the hierarchy of a race-idea can become the locus of meaning for individual and communal existence. Race-ideas are not of necessity exclusionary. A critical point of Voegelin's analysis was that body-ideas (and, by implication, race-ideas) cannot be the sole ideas that inform the order of a community, but that together with other ideas, they are "co-constructors" of the community (*RS*, 14). For Voegelin, body-ideas in a political sense generally assert that the members of a group "are of a common origin" and thereby "integrate [the] group into a substantial whole." Voegelin classified as body-ideas those that had "used [in their] evolution a body-idea in the stricter sense, however far the transformation may have gone." [29]

"The body-idea itself can never be the central idea of a commu-

29. *Ibid.*, 286.

nity" (*RS,* 128). The complex of ideas that order a community may be "more or less complicated," but it can never be founded on a body-idea, or on any single type of idea alone. Presumably, the reason for this is that if a community is to order itself in accordance with the whole of human experience, then it must do so on the basis of ideas stemming at least from each of the major classes of experience. Consequently, body-ideas alone are never a sufficient basis on which to construct a community. Second, given the hierarchy of possibilities within the body-ideas themselves, and the manifold possibilities of combinations with other ideas, there is nothing deterministic about the kind of formative force body-ideas will have in a given community. Certain ones will naturally lend themselves more readily to particular intellectual formations, but not of necessity. Finally, a community is not only a physical entity, but also, and more importantly, an intellectual and spiritual creation. The leading ideas of the community must appeal to the minds and emotions of its members. Consequently, ideas of the mind itself, and of its relation to the personal body and to the analogous body of the community, must be part of the total complex of ideas that shape and establish a community (*RS,* 128).

The most important ideas that we must take into account when considering the combinations of ideas that are effective in erecting political communities are, in fact, the ideas of the mind. It appears in Voegelin's analysis that the theme of the duality of body and mind, which seemed to be the predominant motif in any speculation about the nature of man or the meaning of human experiences, was also an important source of political ideas. The ideas of the mind include ideas of the "individual demon, the intimate communities, and the *Volkgeist*" (*RS,* 67). The importance of mind-ideas for us is that race-ideas, if they are to become effective in the formation of political communities, must incorporate the phenomena of the mind; that is, they must join themselves to mind-ideas. Therefore, when we speak of race-ideas based on a unitary idea of man, we will always see the penetration of mind-ideas into the unitary complex of symbolization that includes body-ideas.

THREE

The Form and Content of the Race-Idea

SUBSTANCE AND PHENOMENA

The essential difference between race-ideas and all other political body-ideas, according to Voegelin, was that race-ideas claimed to be based on "scientific considerations" (*RS,* 8). "Considerations" included the theories and empirical findings of the natural sciences. The junction between natural science and race-idea is race theory, which Voegelin found to be informed by two separate components. The first consisted of the methodologies, epistemologies, concepts, and findings of certain contemporary natural sciences. The second was the idea of race itself, which, distinguished from the political race-idea, was a fundamental image that guided particular researches of the various natural sciences concerned with the study of life. The image was governed in form and substance by the archetype within which it appeared.

Race-ideas and the concept of race must be clearly distinguished from one another. The race-idea is a political symbol that "is used . . . to integrate a community spiritually and politically."[1] As such, it is a part of reality, not a concept, and therefore does not admit of definition, but only of description and theoretical analysis.[2] The race concept, on the other hand, is a concept of the biological and anthropological sciences; it is formally defined and refers to a specific object that, corresponding to its ontological form, is studied according to the formal methods of the respective discipline. Ideally, race theory is the formal discussion of race as a concept. This ideal,

1. Voegelin, "Growth of the Race Idea," 283.
2. For this point, see Voegelin, *The New Science,* 30, and *Autoritäre Staat,* 8.

however, cannot be attained for the reasons to be discussed. Consequently, what we have said about idea and concept with respect to race turns out not to correspond directly to anything that occurs in reality.

Race theory was beset by two interconnected problems: it had a weak basis in philosophical (metaphysical) thought, and it was ruled by a series of scientistic dogmas[3] that precluded the possibility of there ever being a solid philosophical foundation. The former was an inherent weakness introduced in part by the latter, which in turn was a part of race theory because race theorists accepted the epistemological claims of natural scientists without further question.

The analytical object of race theory is man. We have made it clear that Voegelin considered man to be an ontological plurality existing in unity. If this be true, then any science that takes man as its object must either treat the unitary being, or else remain aware that as long as it adheres to a single method pertaining to a single realm of human being, it constitutes a partial treatment of its object. The first dogma of the "scientistic creed" is that "the natural-scientific method is the only one that is 'scientific', and that therefore it alone is called to solve all problems arising on the human horizon" (*RS*, 9). This first dogma has an implied corollary, namely, that the methods of the humanities are not scientific and therefore could neither "solve problems" nor provide us with any real knowledge. Any problems that could not be treated with the methods of the various natural sciences would be considered illusory problems (*Scheinprobleme*).[4] In 1948, Voegelin concluded that the first dogma of scientism implied not only that the *problems* were illusory, but also that the (apparent) phenomena not accessible to the natural sciences were at best irrelevant, and at worst illusory as well.[5] The second major dogma of the natural sciences was that "science moves on a line of continual advance." It was not necessary to know more than the present, particular situation of a specific discipline in order for the scientist to understand his labor as a contribution to the continual accumulation of knowledge. Former problems within the field

3. Voegelin used the term "scientific superstitions" (*wissenschaftliche Superstitionen*) in the German (See *RS*, 8); the English term is also his.

4. Voegelin later distinguished this corollary as a separate dogma. See Eric Voegelin, "The Origins of Scientism," *Social Research*, XV (1948), 462.

5. *Ibid.*, 462.

are "antiquated," and need not concern the researcher (*RS,* 8–9). The two dogmas encourage ignorance regarding genuine theoretical issues related to research and generally impoverish the theoretical depth of scientific study.

I will examine the resulting complex of difficulties in terms of Voegelin's theoretical terminology of substance and phenomenon, first used in 1948. By then, Voegelin's vocabulary had developed sufficiently to make the issues clear in a way that his analytical terms of 1933 did not. This means we must introduce material that is, strictly speaking, beyond the scope of our study, but we may do so because the later discussion exists in nascent form in the writings of 1933. We do not have to bend Voegelin's later concepts to make them fit the framework of our analysis.

The natural sciences are sciences of phenomena, and the humanities (*Geisteswissenschaften*) are sciences of substance. Voegelin extracted arguments concerning the difference between substance and phenomena from the works of Giordano Bruno. Phenomena, the object of the natural sciences, are rooted in physical objects and their relations to one another (force, motion, attraction, etc.). Geometrical descriptions, algebraic formulas, and quantified descriptions are all examples of mathematical expressions pertaining to phenomena. Although anchored in physical entities, they are incidental to the substance or the essence of the entities themselves. The appearance of things, presented to the senses, is not their substance or essence, but exists merely at the "surface of things."

The substance or essence of things is not accessible to the senses, but inheres in reality and is experienced in or by the mind or soul. According to Bruno, it is perceived by a "vision of the spirit." The truth of being, substance, "starts *from* the senses," but is not "*in* the senses": "in the object of the senses it is as in a mirror, in reason it is in the form of argument and discourse, in the intellect in the form of principle and conclusion, and in the spirit it is in its proper and living form."[6] We remember that Voegelin held ideas to be the "real substance that appears as *one* in a *plurality.*" If ideas are a typical example of substance, and an integral part of being that can-

6. Giordano Bruno, "De l'infinito universo e mondi," in *Opere Italiane* (2 vols., Göttingen, 1888), I, 307ff., quoted in Voegelin, "Origins of Scientism," 463.

not be discovered by the senses, then it would seem that we may translate Bruno's statement to mean that the substance of things, namely essence, being, ideas, etc., must be extracted from the phenomena of our senses by what we earlier called the "intellectual activity of analytical removal." Substance includes "man in society and history."[7] Man in society and man in history are not primarily empirical phenomena, but largely configurations of meaning that are created and sustained on the basis of ideas and symbolizations of immediate experiences of (or in) the soul. Consequently, if we study society as we would a phenomenon of the natural sciences, we would find "a stream of human action, articulated by behaviour patterns and purposes of highly questionable unity." If we study the same society in terms of its substance, we will find configurations of meaning, symbols, ideas, and noninstitutional relationships that are the "emotional and volitional substance" that constitute a society in its fullness.[8]

Voegelin was not phobic about the natural sciences, their findings, or their power. Consistent with his ontological and epistemological positions, he argued that natural sciences did have a proper object and that the knowledge of natural science was an important constituent of human knowledge. Biological, anthropological, biochemical, and other studies of man are admissible and even pertinent to political science under certain circumstances, because man is in fact an animal, a mechanism, a biochemical entity, and so forth. Voegelin had no argument with the natural-scientific study of man (RS, 11); his dispute was with the claims of the natural sciences to be exhaustive accounts of the truth of man. The central problem of race theory was that the practitioners and theorists of the natural sciences had a habit of moving beyond their epistemological boundaries into areas where their form of investigation was invalid. As an example of this problem in another discipline, we may mention Voegelin's criticism of the positivist school in legal theory.

Directed largely at the "pure theory of law" of his teacher, Hans Kelsen, Voegelin's analysis of positivism in political science showed that the most important constituents of the political community, political symbols and their meanings, and human relationships and

7. Voegelin, "Origins of Scientism," 463.
8. Voegelin, "Growth of the Race Idea," 284.

their meanings, would be lost to sight in the attempt to study social reality purely in terms of empirical categories. If such a policy were implemented, "then all problems of substance of a theory of the state, and all questions of the constitution of reality would fall away." [9] In other words, the problem with positivistic theories of the state was that if their principles were applied consistently, they would lead us to study the state as a phenomenon rather than as substance. The result would be the kind of empty, physicalist statements about the nature of the state or of other human institutions that we often find in contemporary behavioral social sciences. Such statements indeed exemplify Voegelin's observation that their authors find a "stream of human action articulated by behavior patterns and purposes of highly questionable unity." [10] When we apply the same principles to a study of man, we will dismiss, disregard, or misinterpret those constituent parts of man that are not properly accessible to phenomenal methods of investigation.

"The roots of the state," said Voegelin, "are to be sought in the nature of man" (*RS*, 2). Man, the ontic plurality existing in a unity, will create social entities that correspond to the several ontic classes in which man participates. Consequently, a positivistic theory of the state will be the appropriate vehicle of analysis concerning certain aspects of the reality of the state (*RS*, 6–7). However, other aspects of social or state reality will either be ignored as illusory problems, or they will be deformed in the attempt to appropriate them into ontic classes in which they do not belong. Voegelin found the latter to be the predominant error in positivistic theories of the state;[11] both errors were common in natural-scientific studies of man.

THE BIOLOGICAL STUDY OF MAN

The systematic content of race theory begins with the most important science of living things: biology. Voegelin's discussion of the biological content of race theories is set in the context of a critique of Darwin's theory of the origin of species. The context was dictated by Voegelin's finding that contemporary race-theory was informed in large part by the concepts and claims of Darwinian theory. The

9. Voegelin, *Autoritäre Staat*, 109.
10. We frequently find such descriptions in various systems theories of international relations, or in the models of comparative studies of politics.
11. Voegelin, *Autoritäre Staat*, 103, 113–15.

phenomenon of life is a primordial phenomenon that presents itself in three manners: (1) the living individual entity; (2) the series of individuals that display a constant form; and (3) the "historical unfolding of the living substance in its form-related context." The three manifestations of the primordial phenomena of life are translated in contemporary biology as organism, species, and evolution of life (*RI*, 17).

Charles Darwin was specifically interested in explaining the great diversity of animal species we find on the earth, many of them restricted, in his observation, to very small areas of the planet.[12] Essentially, his explanation consisted of three principles based on two fundamental presuppositions. His first implicit premise was that it made sense to speak of species in the Linnaean meaning of the term;[13] the second was that, all organic forms having a common root, higher forms develop from lower ones.[14] Darwin's three principles were that, first, all individuals vary, however slightly, from all other individuals of a species, including, most importantly, their parents.[15] Second, only those individuals survive that, by virtue of their particular variations in form, can best accommodate themselves to the oftentimes harsh conditions of their environment. By this means, which Darwin called natural selection, only those individuals of a species best adapted to their environment will survive and be able to produce offspring. Third, Darwin assumed that it was possible for parents to pass the traits that enabled them to survive on to their offspring; the traits favored in the process of natural selection could be inherited. On the basis of these three principles, Darwin proposed to explain the origin of all species from a common, primordial ancestor.[16]

Despite Voegelin's dismay at, and contempt for, the general level of theoretical thinking in the natural sciences, considerable portions

12. Erik Nordenskiold, *The History of Biology* (London, 1929), 463; Charles Darwin, *On the Origin of Species by Means of Natural Selection* (New York, 1951), 1.
13. *RS*, 37; Nordenskiold, *History of Biology*, 469.
14. *RS*, 38; Darwin, *Origin of Species*, 285–87.
15. Darwin, *Origin of Species*, 38–45; See *RS*, 38, and F. S. Bodenheimer, *The History of Biology: An Introduction* (London, 1958), 139.
16. Darwin, *Origin of Species*, 53–54, 69–71.

of his critical analysis of Darwinian theory were not new. Not everyone accepted the dogmatic assumptions and claims of the natural sciences as absolute. To begin, Voegelin's observation that Darwin's theory was informed more by the "little-considered dogmas that appealed to the liberal era" than to empirical observations of science (*RS*, 38), was well known, and had been widely discussed since Darwin's time.[17] The dogmatic battles between liberals and conservatives concerning the validity of Darwin's thesis on the basis of their own political beliefs is simply a fact of history.[18]

The core of Darwin's theory and of Voegelin's criticism is the definition of species and individual, and an explanation of their dynamic relationship in the formation of new species. A number of the important details of Voegelin's criticism of Darwin's theory have been raised by others, but his overall approach to the problem is novel. It is related in form to Voegelin's analysis of the theories of consciousness in *Über die Form des amerikanischen Geistes* that we have already considered. A correct understanding of Voegelin's approach to the Darwinian enterprise is necessary for an adequate interpretation of race theory and race-ideas, because the Darwinian conceptions of individual, species, and their relationships lie at the heart of the race theories that are presumed to be the scientific foundation of modern race-ideas. A critical analysis of Darwinian theory in general informs us of the logic and content of race theory. We will follow the form of Voegelin's analysis, but will make reference within that framework to the criticisms others have offered.

Two principles will give us the context of Voegelin's discussion. First, if biology is a natural science, and therefore is the study of phenomena, then the initial task of the biologist is to isolate and define the phenomena he wishes to study. Accordingly, the biological concepts of organism, species, and evolution must all have clear definitions and clearly distinguishable objects or phenomena in empirical reality to which they formally correspond. Second, if life in its "morphological and historical" entirety is one primordial phe-

17. Nordenskiold, *History of Biology,* 458–60, 477–78, 562. See also Charles Singer, *A History of Biology* (New York, 1950), 305, and William Coleman, *Biology in the Nineteenth Century: Problems of Form, Function, and Transformation* (New York, 1971), 87.
18. Nordenskiold, *History of Biology,* 478.

nomenon, but its three parts (individual, series, and biosphere) are distinct phenomena, then the three cannot explain one another, nor can they, taken individually or together, explain the phenomenon of life itself. The principle is the same as the one that governed Voegelin's considerations of theories of consciousness: the parts do not explain the whole, and the whole cannot be explained in terms of a rational system. The whole is a mystery of being. It may be studied, its parts differentiated, and its inherent order analytically articulated, but nothing is thereby explained. The second principle, therefore, is based on the assumption that individual, species, and biosphere refer to ontologically distinct entities or phenomena. The claim that the three manifestations of life are ontologically different is not merely a speculative argument, but is even revealed in biological attempts to explain them theoretically, or at least to describe them in terms of lawlike behavior. The laws of species development and constancy contradict one another, so that "the more we concentrate on the one, the more inconceivable the other becomes" (*RI,* 19). The two apparently contradictory laws both describe phenomena that are a part of the same larger phenomenon. This problem will reappear presently.

Darwin's theory of the origin of species is an example of an attempt to explain the unexplainable, and to do so with concepts that do not directly correspond to any empirical phenomena. Voegelin saw Darwinism as a primary example of replacing "the simple view of the primordial phenomenon" with a theory (*RI,* 18). We can see, without a theory, "that there is a substance in the world that has form and is able to transform itself into another form." This is evident from seeing reproduction within a species, noting the morphological relatedness of various species, and examining the paleontological record that seems to demonstrate a "chronology of forms." A theory that wants to explain all these phenomena is searching for a law behind the developmental law that is displayed in the "inherent unfolding of the living substance" itself; it is trying to explain "a phenomenon that we must accept as unexplained" (*RI,* 18). Voegelin narrowed the problem even further. "All attempts at explanation," he wrote, "are born of the desire to reduce the phenomenon of life to a law of inorganic nature, or, expressed ontologically, they deny the reality of life and see as the only primordial phenomenon, which is to explain all others, inanimate matter." [19] The theoretical enterprise is beset with a number of difficulties that are closely connected to its misbegotten attempt to explain the unexplainable.

Darwin himself noted the vagueness of the terms that appeared to be central to his theory. "No one definition" of species had "as yet satisfied all naturalists," wrote Darwin. The "term 'variety'," the source of speciation, was "almost equally as difficult to define." [20] Even at a much later date, *species* was still the "most abstract term in biology and the most difficult to define," and its lack of a "clear definition . . . one of the weakest points in the present state of biological science." [21] The precise nature of the vagueness of the term *species* may best be articulated in an examination of Voegelin's discussion of it and the term *individual*.

The concept of process seems to have been essential in Voegelin's interpretations of the phenomenon of life, and will help us to understand his analysis of Darwinian theory and its concepts. Voegelin conceived of all three levels of the manifestation of life to be in process at the same time that they could be identified as belonging to distinct, apparently static, ontological classes. A species, whatever it may be, is made up of individuals, so Voegelin began with the single, living entity as the fundamental building-block of Darwin's theory. The individual, perceived at first sight to be a static, physical entity with definite exterior and interior, exists in process with its environment; it takes in material that is processed and becomes part of itself at the same time that it excretes material that was once part of itself as a living entity, and now becomes part of the "external" environment again (*RS*, 40).

Second, individuals mature and then decline toward old age, both physically and, at least for humans and the more complex animals, mentally. Therefore, when we speak of identity, we are trying to isolate a certain "something" that extends through time, and which is difficult if not impossible to isolate empirically. But it is only if we believe that there is a core of identity in every individual person that attributing personality (and in the communal world), responsibility, praise, and blame to humans, and attributing personality or

19. *RI*, 18. See also *RS*, 46.
20. Darwin, *Origin of Species*, 38; see also 273.
21. Nordenskiold, *History of Biology*, 469; Singer, *A History of Biology*, 467.

an identity alone to animals, have any meaning. Whatever the core of identity within the individual biological process may be, it is not discovered in phenomenal studies: identity is a matter of essence.

Third, when the individual is reduced to its origins, the germ cells, we find that even these cannot provide us with what we seek, namely the boundaries of the material, extended (in the Cartesian sense) individual. The germ cells can be traced back to the parents, where they become internal, rather than external, entities that are once again developed in a material process encompassing both "inner" and "outer" materials. Consequently, "individuals are not closed entities, but periodic knots in the continual line of organic substance. The boundary of the individual is . . . crossed over into the parents" (*RS*, 41). Defining individuals in terms of their genetic composition is not a solution to this problem because, first, identifying individual genetic material suffers from the same theoretical difficulties that we find in trying to identify phenomenally the individual living entity; and second, individuals are not merely "a puzzle of hereditary factors," but living entities, unified and indivisible in form and appearance, at the same time that they are linked in a historical chain (*RS*, 51).

Finally, within the evolutionary theory of the origin of species, when the inner-outer problem is traced to its ultimate origin, there is a point at which an outer inorganic material spontaneously transforms itself into an inner-outer phenomenon, the inner having an inherent, organic nature governed by laws of organic process not evidenced in the outer, inorganic substance. The distinction between an animate entity and its environment is lost in this final step. The problem of origins thereby becomes "the boundary problem of inner-outer speculation." The "absolute end of the speculative continuum" is the "leap" between organic and inorganic nature, which can be "covered up in various ways by zealous thinkers" (*RS*, 46). Voegelin pointed out that this speculative problem was in form the same as the mind-body speculations that resulted in the various constructions we have already outlined. Organic and inorganic substance are dissimilar in their inherent order, but also cross over into one another. To let one arise from the other results in familiar constructions in which, in this case, the inorganic realm and its order become an epiphenomenon of the inorganic. Once again, the ontological duality, if it is to retain any meaningful content, must remain a mystery that cannot be penetrated by rational systems (or their natural-scientific equivalents, theories) (*RS,* 47).

This analysis of the concept of the individual showed that in terms of Darwin's theory, individuals do not transmit characteristics, etc., from one to another, but that as "knots on the continual line of organic substance," they and their characteristics are the "existential persistence of a chemically and physically determined, structured substance" (*RS,* 41). Furthermore, Voegelin demonstrated that the distinction between individual and environment, vital to the Darwinian concept of natural selection, was not tenable in its pure form. External environment and internal individual are speculative concepts that correspond to seeing the individual living entity and its environment as a primordial phenomenon, but that do not empirically correspond to concrete phenomena that we could examine with the phenomenal methods of science. Voegelin's conclusion was that "individual" was not an indivisible entity that could serve as the phenomenal foundation of a theory of the origins of species, but that it was a "speculative-dialectical concept" (*RS,* 42). It is speculative because it is not an "empirical concept . . . that faithfully signifies some well-isolatable contents or traits," but a description of an identity that we see in the manifold instances of its unfolding (*RS,* 42). Nevertheless, the living form is a primordial phenomenon; "the living entity placed into an environment, the subject in its medium, is an indubitable reality" (*RS,* 42). It is dialectical because the individual is not indivisible, but is constituted in a continual line of ascendants and descendants, and is an entity in continual material process. "Individual" does not signify a static entity, but a temporally bounded continuum in existence. Dialectically, "individual" is the moment of a process of becoming, at the same time that it contains the order of that becoming.

Voegelin's analysis of species as an empirical concept followed the same four steps as his critique of the concept of individual. In the same way that the individual exists in a reciprocal, interwoven relationship with its environment, the characteristics of a species that are determined by environment and those that are genotypical are intertwined and difficult to separate. The relationship of species and environment introduces the problem of variation, about which we may say two things. First, only hereditary variations, that is, variations that persist in the continual line of the species' organic substance, are significant for determining the nature of species.[22] Second, even when we examine only these characteristics, we find that if the genetic mass were not structured in such a way that the environmental conditions were effective in precisely the way that they are, then the "particular modifications and adaptive appearances would be impossible." The reverse of this is that we find that genotypical changes in the genetic mass of the species are caused by environmental conditions. Thus, "the difference between hereditary and non-hereditary variations cannot be traced back to the opposition of interior and exterior as if to a final resting-place, but it receives its support from the 'seen' phenomena of constancy, fluctuation, and variation of the 'seen' types" (RS, 43).

Following the second step of the analysis of individual, species, according to Darwin, are in continual transition. One must then ask what, if it is in a continual state of flux, a species might be. What are the phenotypical and genotypical boundaries that differentiate one species from another? What is the core of identity, the essence of a species, if the traits and characteristics of its members are not only not identical with one another, but moreover, are continually changing as a whole?

In terms of origins, a species has no empirical external-internal boundaries if it is a moment in the historical unfolding of organic substance since the first life-form arose from wherever it did. It is a momentary manifestation of a continuity of fluid form that, according to post-Darwinian theory, arose spontaneously out of inanimate matter. A species is neither a closed entity with respect to other species, nor, at its root, with respect to the external, inanimate environment. The same arguments may be applied to the "living substance" (the biosphere) in general.

Voegelin's analysis of Darwinian concepts of species and individual have some similarities to Zeno's paradoxes. If species, as used in Darwin's apparent double meaning, is both an identifiable, static phenomenon at the same time that it is in continual process, we have a problem similar in form to the paradox of reconciling moment and rate. The advance of a turtle toward a wall, or an arrow in flight, can be considered in terms of discrete proportions, but because the pro-

22. Nordenskiold, *History of Biology,* 467.

portions are infinitely divisible, we find that the advance of the turtle or the arrow cannot be expressed in terms of arithmetic fractions. It may also be considered in terms of rate, which ignores the discrete, infinitesimal moments of the line of advance, and expresses movement in terms of flow rather than moment. The moments of the advance can never be isolated (though we can isolate segments of moments) because they are always further divisible, but the rate of advance is a visible, empirical phenomenon that can be mathematically (*i.e.,* lawfully) expressed. The same problem appears to be true of the process of conscious, physical sense-perception, which can be broken down into infinitesimal units of force so that its continuity disappears, at the same time that its nature as a process remains experientially intact. Similarly, it is possible empirically to study the nature of the process of becoming of an individual, a species, or the biosphere, but it is not possible empirically to isolate the moments of the process at any of the three levels. Consequently, Voegelin concluded that the concepts used in modern theories of evolution were based on a speculative theorizing that was prior to any formulation of theories, or to any empirical investigations. This objection to a kind of reification of the symbols used to describe reality was not formulated to prevent the theoretical use of the idea of individual, but to keep it from being misidentified as an empirical concept (remembering that it could still be used as a *theoretical* concept). Awareness of its speculative nature put theories of evolution and modern theories of race, which were based in part on the former, in a proper theoretical perspective. As has been the case with several phenomena we have studied so far, individual and species are both seen phenomena that ultimately cannot be traced to an immutable, concrete (*i.e.,* material) core that we can handle and label as *the* object of our investigations. Both phenomena are *real,* but not in the reified way that theorists of race, deriving their theories from the hypotheses of empirical science, would assume.

The problem with "defining" both species and individual is that both display a constancy of type (the moment) and also variation (the process) in their morphological and genetic structure from individual to individual (ascendant to descendant). Therefore, whatever the organic substance may be, constancy and variation appear to be part of the "function of [its] structure" in its "becoming in an environment" (*RS*, 44). It turns out that individual and species, as we have discovered them to be used here, are not empirical concepts at all, but *ideas*. They are symbols for the "unity in a plurality," the identity that encompasses the whole at the three distinct levels of the phenomenon of life. They could not be empirical concepts, because they symbolize two opposite phenomena that exist in a unity. Consequently, their phenomenal articulation in terms of scientific laws contradicts itself at every step (laws of constancy oppose laws of variation). It is possible to symbolize theoretically a duality that exists in a unity (duality-in-unity being one such symbol), but the only way symbolically to reconcile the reality of two concrete, distinct ontological phenomena that inhere in a concrete, individual entity, or a group of them, is to unite them in an *idea,* an expression of the contradictory essence of the entity itself. But the phenomenal sciences cannot function by using such metaphysical symbolization. In order for species to become a phenomenon that permits an empirical study of its inherent order, we must remove the phenomenal contradiction, isolating one aspect or the other as the phenomenal reality of a species. Clearly, its constancy, and even its variation within certain constant limits, are easier objects of investigation than its process of variation and change. Since species embodied both aspects of its nature in Darwin's conception, species as a natural-scientific concept failed; it had to fail because it was an idea.

Voegelin, therefore, found that the Mendelian and post-Mendelian investigations of the hereditary laws of species, that is, their laws of constancy, had come to "excellent results." It would appear that in accordance with the strictures of natural-scientific epistemology, Mendelian laws mathematically described empirical phenomena. The problem of mutation and variation, on the other hand, largely due to difficulties in experimentally determining anything about it, had not seen progress since Darwin's time (*RS*, 44). The matter does not end here.

Two related responses to Darwin's theory were made within the discipline of biology in an attempt to explain the constancy and variation of species at the same time. Both categories of theoretical responses to the problem proposed that organic substance was characteristically predisposed toward mutating only in specific directions. In each case, a quasiteleological principle either within or "behind" the organic substance, whether influenced by environmental factors or not, would be the source of all variation. Species could then be defined in terms of the parameters of reaction and change established by its inherent principle of order and unfolding.

The essential difference between the two kinds of theoretical speculation centered upon whether (1) the principles of constancy and variation were immanent in the organic material itself and could be reduced to some kind of material order, or (2) the principles were functions of a vital force, ontologically distinct from organic substance, regardless of whether organic substance could be reduced to the cells, the genes, or the chromosomes, or be considered as the entire organism itself. Unfortunately, the debate between proponents of the two types of theory has usually been described within the framework of a dogmatic conflict between vitalists and mechanists.[23] The deeper, theoretical stances of either theory often seemed to be irrelevant; the choice between the one side and the other was ideological, perhaps a matter of taste. Disputes of this kind end rational discussion and reduce the debate to a struggle between armed camps.

In strictly dogmatic terms, Voegelin was a vitalist. He did not believe that an immanentized conception of life adequately addressed the problems of material transfer, growth, transformation, functional harmony, regeneration, and death that we see as some of the phenomena arising only in organic, not inorganic, matter. Mechanists regarded organic matter as a reactive substance "that is in a reciprocal relationship with other, external substance," so that there is no essential difference between the two. Animate phenomena thereby become epiphenomena of the inanimate. Given the apparent ontological differences in their structure, function, and order, Voegelin found this doctrine untenable (*RS,* 50–51); a "material substructure for the inherited dispositions"[24] could not become the locus of life and its laws of becoming.

If Voegelin's Kantian epistemological assertion that only material phenomena can be treated by natural-scientific methods holds true, then we encounter the same difficulty we have already addressed several times. Vitalist "explanations" of life are theoretical speculations about the immaterial substratum that is ontologically distinct

23. See *ibid.,* 603–16, and Singer, *A History of Biology,* 37.
24. Nordenskiold, *History of Biology,* 563; also 555–56.

from the material of the organism, and that appears to order the material processes of the individual in such a way that we can speak of a nonmaterial essence of identity of the given organism. Therefore, "the concept of an identical constant is necessitated by the continuation of the analysis that wants to maintain the unity [existing] in the exchange of the anabolic material" (*RS*, 50). The constant that is the essence of the organism is no possible object of a natural science; it is an idea, an essence. This realization puts Voegelin and those like him (but not vitalists) beyond the pale of dogma or ideology. As for materialists:

> It is not, then, the idea—in itself justifiable—of limiting discussion to the chemical and physical manifestations of the phenomena of life that constitute the weakness of these mechanistic theories of life, but the stubborn insistence upon the rough comparisons between phenomena in animate and inanimate nature—comparisons in fact, the weakness of which would undoubtedly be realized by their proponents if the latter were not really trying all the time to lay the foundations of some kind of general philosophical theory extending far beyond the bounds of natural science.[25]

Coincidentally summarizing what Voegelin was showing in his examination of biological science, Nordenskiold here penetrates to the heart of the dogmatic debate between vitalists and mechanists. He also traces an important line of intent from biological theories to race theories, which in fact always contain a political component.

The proposition of a nonmaterial principle is a logical conclusion from the material, but animate, phenomena that scientists can investigate *qua* scientists. Attempts to "explain" the observable, describable, and analyzable "material process in the living organism or its parts" in terms of "known material processes in inanimate nature" is not possible: "those who have attempted to do so have either reverted to gross schematism or else drawn a bill on the possible progress of tomorrow."[26] Aside from the intellectual dishonesty of such cheerful, but unfounded, optimism, it ignores the ontological and epistemological objections outlined in this and the previous chapter. Such dishonesty probably is not primarily engendered by an optimistic mood, but by a desire to transgress the boundaries of

25. *Ibid.*, 607.
26. *Ibid.*

anthropological studies that dealt with man on the level of race. Three observations may be gleaned from Voegelin's discussion. First, race as a means of classification is not so empirically rigorous as was species in the biological search for the "pure line." Race is defined as a "complex of characteristics" that distinguish one group of individuals from other groups with different sets of characteristics (*RS,* 57). Although some anthropologists attempted to select only characteristics that could be inherited, thereby uniting anthropology and genetics, selecting such characteristics within the methodological limits of anthropology proved impossible. Consequently, the complex of characteristics that delimits (to avoid using "defines") a race is made up of both hereditary and environmentally induced characteristics (*RS,* 58).

Second, there are no precise rules for delimiting the kinds of characteristics and traits that distinguish the races, nor is there an exact methodology by which races may be distinguished. Although some anthropologists tried to disclaim it, the underlying basis of selecting traits and characteristics and delimiting races is that certain "combinations of traits and characteristics attract the observer's attention" (*RS,* 61). In the words of Eugen Fischer, the selecting of traits is governed by "experience" (*RS,* 60). Which of the traits are hereditary, and which are largely determined by a particular environment, is both irrelevant and undiscoverable. It is irrelevant because anthropologically, race cannot be defined in terms of human genetics; it is undiscoverable, because, in any event, we cannot experimentally breed humans for a number of generations to extract the purely genetic factors (*RS,* 42).

Third, the anthropological understanding of race frequently transcends the purely somatic sphere that is the field of investigation for biology. When a complex of characteristics "becomes noteworthy," it will usually include certain mental characteristics that become part of the habitus of a group, which is what is noticed by the anthropologist and informs his delimitations of the racial group (*RS,* 59, 61). It appears that already at this stage, mind and body are joined in theoretical speculation and in systematic classifications.

Combining Voegelin's three observations, we find that the notion of *habitus* becomes the underlying epistemological unity of the activities and speculations of anthropologists. The word itself, a rare medical term in English, signifies a deportment, bearing, set of behaviors, disposition, or character in the meaning intended here. According to Baldwin, the term received its anthropological meaning in German via zoology, where it referred to "all specific actions of animals whether instinctive or acquired." [30] The use of this term as a symbol for the perceived behavioral and morphological unity of a group indicates the introduction of a considerable amount of what we earlier called substance into a purportedly phenomenal study. The habitus is an *idea* of classification that is "nothing more than the observed constancy of traits and their combinations" (*RS*, 62). Characteristics and traits that attract the attention of the "experienced" observer embody the anthropological idea of a race. Consequently, "purity" of race is relative to the system of classification (*RS*, 62). The introduction of habitus as the constituent element of race was a sign that mental and spiritual characteristics were unquestionably considered part of the race-idea.

The most important point of Voegelin's discussion of anthropological concepts of race was that though certain anthropologists attempted to attach their notion of race to the genetic definition of race as a "pure line" in biology, such a union was impossible. (The authoritative importance of genetics in particular was that it was and is the modern locus of investigation into the laws of morphological formation and heredity.) The impossibility of the union, and the nontheoretical nature of species, apart from its narrow, experimental meaning as a "pure line," did not stop some biologists and anthropologists from maintaining that such a connection did, in fact, exist, or from continuing their discussions of race as if that union existed. Consequently, the dividing line between the concept and the idea of race is indistinct, and easily crossed by the thoughtless, the unwary, or the mendacious. The anthropological "concept" of race, which is really an idea of race, thereby takes on an aura of the authoritativeness of a natural-scientific concept. The "inauthentic thinking" engendered by this sleight-of-hand matures fully in race theory.

30. James Mark Baldwin (ed.), *Dictionary of Philosophy and Psychology* (3 vols., Gloucester, 1957), I, 435.

FOUR

The Classification and Theory of Race

In the course of his investigations, Voegelin discovered that the race-idea had had a long history in intellectual speculation. In *Die Rassenidee in der Geistesgeschichte* he gave a history, or better, a genealogy, of the race-idea, focusing primarily on its role in biological speculation. Voegelin's study was a history of biology, but distinguished from most others in that it was a discussion of biological thought and speculation at the level of ideas, rather than of dogma, method, discovery, etc. He did not use a developmental or, in the sense used by Thomas Kuhn, a revolutionary, model, but rather, traced the genesis and transformation of a particular idea.

Voegelin's account of the race-idea and its transformation consisted of two parallel discussions, each of which dealt with the three aspects in which the primordial phenomenon of life presented itself. We are already familiar with them: the living individual entity, the series of individuals that display a constant form, and the historical unfolding of the living substance in its form-related context. The parallel discussions consider human and nonhuman life (at the level of human life, the "historical unfolding of the living substance" becomes mankind, and the series of constant forms becomes the race, or subspecies); at the same time, a constant and essential theme is the place of man in the realm of life in general.

Voegelin held all three aspects of the larger phenomenon of life to be primal phenomena themselves at the same time as they were three "manners of appearing" of the former (*RI*, 18). We have already shown that the three primal manifestations of life do not explain one another, nor need to be explained at all. Based on our earlier argument concerning the nature of archetypes and their relationship to the primal phenomena, we know that the form of interpretation and symbolization is a result of a particular primal manner of seeing these primal phenomena. It is possible, then, for the perspective of the primal manner of seeing to change, and for us to trace this change by examining the symbolic images of the basic phenomena and their content.

Die Rassenidee in der Geistesgeschichte is the study of a fundamental change in the perspective of seeing the primal phenomena, traced partially through the change in symbolization, and partially through the transformation of the systematic content of formally identical symbols. The two archetypes that are transformed correspond to Voegelin's two parallel accounts: the phenomenon of life and the nature of man. The transformation of the archetypes and the alteration of the systematic content of the three phenomena of which they are composed is a reciprocal relationship. Examination of the three phenomena and a change of mind about their form, constitution, or inherent order may influence one to alter one's perspective concerning one of the larger archetypes, either of the nature of life itself, or of human nature. Conversely, a change in one primal perspective may unexpectedly alter one's interpretation of certain phenomena occurring within the boundaries of the larger, archetypical phenomenon.

The breadth of material that Voegelin covered was immense. He himself contended that the difficulty and magnitude of the task precluded many people, especially theorists of race, from engaging themselves in an understanding of the meaning of race, its genealogy, and its theoretical problems (*RI*, 23). The list of thinkers and researchers included Linnaeus, Kant, Leibniz, Goethe, Herder, Buffon, Wolff, and numerous others. Voegelin followed the thread through botany, experimental biology, and speculative biology to the highest theoretical levels of philosophy. He saw the task of tracing the genealogy not merely as an academic exercise that would expand the "horizon of knowledge." Such a genealogy, rather, "pursues the scientifically practical goal of recalling the basic archetypical and iconic questions that have at present disappeared from consideration, of establishing them anew and of encouraging further work on them" (*RI*, 23).

Given the magnitude of the work, though it is only 150 pages in length, I will not attempt to provide a detailed consideration of the whole, nor is one necessary for our present purposes. Instead, I will outline the two basic themes central to Voegelin's understanding of the modern notion of race. They are (1) the transformation of a transcendent conception of life in general into an immanent image of it, and (2) a concomitant transformation of the image of human existence as transcendent to one that portrays human life and nature to be wholly immanent. What this transformation means, and how it is symbolized will be the focus of the discussion. I omit most of Voegelin's genealogical tracing, retaining only enough to make clear the questions he sought to recover. Modern theories of race are based on an idea of the immanent person.

This summary of Voegelin's argument will help us understand the primal manner of seeing that supports the speculative enterprises of modern race theory. We assumed a number of premises about the nature of life in the previous chapter, which Voegelin's genealogy showed were based on archetypes of life rather than purely theoretical arguments. In this regard, we are reminded of the arguments presented in the first chapter, that the archetype and philosophical accounts of it are *reciprocally* related.

THE TRANSCENDENTAL ARCHETYPE

CLASSIFICATION SYSTEMS AND THEORIES OF GENERATION

We have seen that race and species are ideas that refer to the unity we find in a plurality of individuals. The idea of race or species is always related to the problem of generation, it seems, because the phenomenon symbolized in the idea of species is the unity of a group of discrete individuals that appear to be related to one another in accordance with a lawlike succession of generation, and with respect to their common form.[1] It has been known since ancient times that like begets like, and only two "likes" beget anything at all, with the exception of a few limited (and sterile) interspecies exemplars.[2] The goal of much biological speculation has been to ex-

1. In the words of Nordenskiold, "A species is regarded as the sum total of those individuals which resemble one another as though they had a common origin." Nordenskiold, *History of Biology,* 212.
2. For example, for a discussion of the meaning of the Hebrew *miyn,* or "kind," see C. F. Keil and F. Delitzsch, *The Pentateuch* (Grand Rapids, 1981),

plain the complex of phenomena and problems that reside in this basic bit of knowledge. The quest for an explanation begins with the realization that it is possible to order all living entities in nature into a system of groups on the basis of certain criteria that establish the unifying characteristics of each group. Attempts at systematic classification of the diverse phenomena of the biosphere are at least as old as the pre-Socratic Greeks.[3]

The subtlety of Voegelin's reading and understanding are revealed from the first page of his account. He began his discussion with Linnaeus because, in Voegelin's estimation, Linnaeus' system was an example of "convincing simplicity" that was similar to the modern race theories, illustrating some of the same theoretical difficulties. Linnaeus' criterion for differentiating between species was purely morphological. His simple assumption was that God created all the species in the beginning, and that we can recognize the different species on the basis of simple morphological characteristics. "The question of an epistemological theory of living entities and a procedure for their descriptions" were not problems for Linnaeus because of his overwhelming certainty about their origin and nature (*RI*, 26).

In contrast to Linnaeus, Voegelin found a far "deeper treatment" of the problem of species in the writing of two earlier naturalists, John Ray and Francis Willughby. Unlike Linnaeus, both were interested not only in the morphological, but also in the functional, behavioral, and environmental characteristics of species. They were convinced that species could not be differentiated on the basis of morphological characteristics alone.[4]

From an analysis of the theories of Ray and Willughby, and some excursions into the writings of Kant and Goethe, Voegelin showed "the total breadth of the speculative possibilities" of the problem of species in the eighteenth century" (*RI*, 38). Linnaeus looked to one distinguishing physical characteristic at the root of species differentiation, following the scholastic method of classifying species on

---

55–56, 61, Vol. 1 of Keil and Delitzsch, *Commentary on the Old Testament,* and John C. Whitcomb and Henry B. Morris, *The Genesis Flood* (Philadelphia, 1961), 65–67.

3. Nordenskiold, *History of Biology,* 29.

4. *Ibid.,* 200.

the basis of a formal principle, usually morphological in nature.[5] Ray and Willughby, in contrast, sought for a concept of species that did not conform so closely to formal principles as to the reality of nature. In their various formulations, Ray and the other three thinkers took species to be a symbol for a *complex* of characteristics, that seen together would constitute a species (*RI*, 27). The concepts of the "essence," "total habitus" (to use Voegelin's term), or their equivalents, became the center of any speculation about the nature of species in theoretically more insightful systems of classification. Voegelin considered Ray's concept of essence to be equivalent to Woltereck's concept of the "norm of reaction," both in what is described and in its double meaning: "Ray's essence signifies at the same time the cause of the organic form in the fullness of its features, and the seen nature of the living creature that serves as the basic idea for the selection of the features through which the living entity is to be 'essentially' or 'naturally' described" (*RI*, 33).

The concept of type that is developed to define a species in terms of its essence, like the concept of the norm of reaction, allows for certain deviations from the conceptual standard that do not require the classifier to contrive new species for every instance of a morphological, behavioral, etc., difference. The most fundamental criterion for establishing the boundaries of a species between individuals and groups of individuals is whether or not the members can interbreed, producing fertile offspring (*RI*, 30, 38). Together with the criterion of the "perceived unity" of the members of a group, we have fairly closely described the outer limits of speculation about classifying species in the eighteenth century and, in most respects, in the present day. Voegelin favoured Ray's presentation over that of Linnaeus because the former neither defended a particular position, nor attempted to "solve" the problems that arose from his empirical investigations, but was able to identify the theoretical problems of the origin of species, the method of identifying and describing species, and of the continuity of species that Linnaeus either passed over, or responded to by dogmatic simplification (*RI*, 80). Voegelin did not share the high opinion that many hold of the so-called "father of systematic classification."[6]

5. *Ibid.*, 207–208.
6. For a comparison of Voegelin's evaluation with that of prevailing opinion,

Having established the systematic principles for setting the manifold of living entities into a series of related categories, how are we to explain the existence of the categorically related individuals in nature, and in their apparent generation from one another? Specifically, how shall we explain the continuity of species over a number of generations of individuals? Voegelin divided all explanations into two groups: the immanentist and transcendentalist. "All attempts to explain the unity of life through divine creation and the encapsulation of all successive generations in the one originally created, as well as the mechanical theories of the origin of life, are transcendent; all interpretations, however, that see life as an ontic realm with its own nature, and that assume a vital agent, in kind like Herder's genetic force, through which the character of the living entity is determined, are immanentist." Transcendental explanations took either "God or the inanimate mechanical natural occurrence" as their starting-point of explanation (*RI*, 38). Two basic theories, the theory of epigenesis and the theory of pre-formation embody these two types of transcendental explanation of the continuity of species.

The theory of epigenesis explained the generation of new living entities in terms of a chemical process, in which the new individual grew out of the materials provided to it in the womb or in the egg. Generation was described by William Harvey as a "process of growth and formation carried on at the same time."[7] René Descartes described it as a process of fermentation (*RI*, 82). Neither Harvey nor Descartes perceived the principle of formation and growth to inhere in the organic material itself. It was unclear to Harvey wherein the governing principle did inhere, though he appears to have rejected explanations that "involved a controlling mind or soul." Descartes, likewise, did not perceive the ordering of material to arise out of the material itself.[8]

---

see *RI*, 26, and Nordenskiold, *History of Biology*, 210. The theoretical aspects of biological speculation did not appear to be so worrisome to Nordenskiold, who is considered an authority in the field of historical biology, as they were to Voegelin.

7. William Harvey, "On Animal Generation," in R. Willis, (trans., ed.), *The Works of William Harvey* (London, 1847), 338, cited in Elizabeth G. Gasking, *Investigations into Generation, 1651–1828* (Baltimore, 1967), 30.

8. Gasking, *Investigations into Generation*, 34; René Descartes, "Tractatus de formatione foetus," in *Opera Omnia* (6 vols.; Amsterdam, 1686), III, xxviii, cited in *RI*, 82.

The second transcendentalist theory, the theory of pre-formation, held that the living entity existed with all its parts in microscopic form in the ovum, or, in some versions of the theory, partially in the ovum, and partially in the sperm. There are several other variations of this particular theory; I have given its basic form here. The theory accounted for the phenomenon of the gradual appearance of a living entity from unformed matter, since we could now say that the form existed from the beginning of the process of growth, and merely accrues material to itself in the process. Later versions based on parts from both sexes also accounted for the common experience that offspring usually acquire characteristics from both parents. The pre-formation theorists were perhaps somewhat more open about their transcendent theorizing: they speculated that God had originally organized inanimate matter into living entities at creation, and that He had encapsulated all future generations in the germ cells of the original parents: "It followed from such a view that there was no true generation; what appeared as the formation of a new individual was simply the growth of an organized living thing which had been formed at the beginning of time." [9] Voegelin considered both theories to be transcendentalist, because both postulated that "the principle of becoming" of the living entity did not lie in the entity itself, but that the entity was considered a machine or a mechanism whose principle of formation lay outside itself (RI, 80).

In very brief form, we have outlined Voegelin's discussion of the two different principles of the classification of species, and the predominant theories of generation up to about 1759. We see that, on the level of nonhuman life, the biosphere in general unfolds according to predestined, transcendent principles that have determined the order and diversity of the living world from the beginning. Species are generally considered to be static insofar as they do not transmute into new species. [10] In the encapsulation version of the pre-formation theory, at least, the individual entity has been created and determined at the beginning of time.

Since man is a living being, part of the discipline of biology is to

9. Gasking, *Investigations into Generation*, 42.
10. Voegelin noted that Ray was somewhat hesitant about the static unfolding of species, but even if new species did arise after the original act of creation, this would still involve a direct, creative act of God. See John Ray, *Three Physico-theological discourses* (4th ed.; London, England, 1732), 48, cited in *RI*, 36.

understand at least the biological nature of man (assuming that his intellectual and spiritual natures are matters separate from biological investigation), and to integrate man into the biological systems of classification and theories of generation. We need not say much about the speculation on the origin of man during the period with which we are presently concerned. In epigenetic theories, men were considered to form in the womb in the same way that mammals were, so that the foetus formed in conformity to the lawful chemical processes of its respective species, *Homo sapiens*. According to the "classic" version of pre-formationist theory, Eve was thought to contain all future individuals of the human race in her original ova, which she then passed on to her descendants in a continual line of disencapsulation up to the present time (*RI*, 81).

THE CLASSIFICATION OF MAN

The classification of man may be divided into two parts. In the first instance, we must decide how we shall integrate man into the whole of the biosphere; in the second, we must develop principles and methods for differentiating among the various varieties, subspecies, or races of men.

Voegelin showed through the classification schemes of Buffon and Linnaeus that the greatest difficulty in classifying man within the animal kingdom, given the general opinion of their time about man's status in comparison to the animals, was that in order to integrate a being who was thought of as above the animals, having a thinking and spiritual nature different from them, this nature had to be separated from his physical, animal nature. Consequently, a premise of any classification under these restrictions had to be that the classifier would accept the kinds of segmentary construction of human nature with which we are already familiar. The segmentary constructions allowed man to be integrated into the lower echelons of biological systems without affecting his intellectual or spiritual status. Buffon based his segmentary constructions on a vulgar Cartesian dualism, and Linnaeus, according to Voegelin, did not particularly concern himself with the theorctical problems of his method of classification one way or another (*RI*, 39, 44). But in his naïveté he confused the two ontic realms in his delineation of the characteristics by which man would be classified in the general classification of all living entities (*RI*, 46).

Having, on the basis of a segmentary construction, classified

man in the order of all life, we still face the problem of differentiating the various apparent subspecies of men. We mentioned earlier
that a great impetus behind the schemes to classify the manifold
races was the wealth of travelogues and historical accounts that
reached their numerical zenith in the eighteenth century. The classification schemes that Voegelin discussed are best divided into two
categories.

The first category comprises those systems that are attempts to
classify the races of man purely on the basis of physical phenomena,
including characteristics of the body, geography, and climate (the
latter two insofar as they affect the form of the body). In accordance
with the segmentary construction of man's nature, the proponents of
these theories ignored, as far as possible, the intellectual and spiritual components of race, and isolated the physical components of
man's nature as the determinants for classifying individuals according to race. The second category contains those systems of classification that admit the unitary nature of man, and classify the various
races in accordance with this acknowledgment. Thus, cultural and
sociopolitical factors become part of the criteria for describing and
classifying races. According to Voegelin, neither approach was entirely successful, each for a different reason.

Buffon's system of classification was Voegelin's first example of
the first kind of system. Through it Voegelin showed that the unity
of man's nature continually crept into descriptions and classifications that purported to be entirely physical in scope; thus, "we already find here the first attempts to cover the description of the empirically found psychophysical human types that are determined as
human unitary forms by the mind, with a purely natural-scientific
explanation of the somatic manifold." Voegelin continued, "This
explanation does not fully cover up the psychic phenomenon, as in
some modern theories of race," since man's nature is still seen in his
reason by the author of the system (*RI*, 57). Methodologically,
Buffon's classification is "impure," because it wavered between the
ontic realms of which man is constituted. At one point, man was
classified according to his physical characteristics; and at another,
the external influences that determine racial characteristics were described in terms of their influence on the mind in its constituting role
as part of race (*RI*, 58). Blumenbach's and Kant's systems were the
other two exemplars of physical classification based on a segmentary construction. They are theoretically more sound because their

authors were aware of the epistemological and methodological difficulties surrounding a definition of race. In both systems, man was differentiated from animals on the basis of his reason (*RI*, 66). Because of their theoretical exactness, Kant and Blumenbach were consistently able to apply physical criteria as the differentiation between races without merging them into the realm of the mind.

Herder's system, the last example under the present archetype of nature and man, was chosen because it showed the beginnings of a different kind of speculative construction of man's nature that allowed one to classify man in the realm of nature and with respect to various races on the basis of his whole being, not just a segment of it. Herder seemed at first glance to treat man as a holistic being. All of man's ontic nature, according to Voegelin's interpretation of him, had to be considered when determining and classifying racial characteristics. In accordance with the fourth type of speculative construction outlined in Chapter Two, in Herder's system the body is permeated by the mind, and becomes a field of expression of it. The influences of climate and geography on the mind, for example, are major determinants of race both in its psychic characteristics, including language and culture, and in some of its physical characteristics. The latter become doubtful criteria for a classification of race in Herder's conception (*RI*, 79).

Herder did not classify the races according to characteristics that he considered to be given as differentiating traits in the nature of the races themselves, but he classified them in accordance with conventional criteria that he did not consider to have any consequences in reality. The classification of races did not conform to ontologically "real" criteria that constituted an inherent reason for making divisions, but was made along arbitrarily chosen lines for the sake of convenience. For this reason, Herder spoke of *Volk*, referring to a "human collective" that is delineated in terms of the psychic characteristics of culture and language, and on the basis of geography, rather than on the basis of any neobiological claims (*RI*, 63–64)

Ultimately, according to Voegelin, Herder retreated from this unitary construction and showed himself to belong in his speculation to the segmentary form. Unlike the rest of the created world, in which creatures fulfull their existence as unitary entities in their existence itself, man is an "intermediate creature" that stands between animals and a form of being higher than himself. His destiny is fulfilled in the "unfolding" of the "pure mind," not in his bodily, or even psychophysical, existence (*RI*, 61). Although the meaning of individual life becomes this-worldly—the mind "unfolds" here, in this world, and is not being perfected in a realm in the Beyond—Herder calls upon God to provide the meaning for immanent existence, so that the meaning of man's life is ultimately tied to a transcendent source.[11] In spite of this essentially transcendent conception of the nature of human existence, Voegelin pointed to Herder's speculations as one of the first indicators of a turning-point in the archetypical transformation of the race-idea. The second, more obviously transcendent aspect of Herder's system was that the standard of classification did not inhere in the classified phenomena themselves, but was imposed from without. Species and race could not be ontologically "real," but were rational constructs of the human mind.

The picture Voegelin has drawn for us of the archetype of nature up to the end of the eighteenth century may be briefly summarized. The predominant image of life is based on a segmentary construction type (*RI*, 79). All living entities are considered to be machines or mechanisms empowered by a vital force that is separate from the essence of the mechanism itself. It is possible to order the entire realm of living things into a series of groups, based on a number of (generally) physical criteria. The world and its inhabitants are finite. There is a definite beginning of creation, at which time all things were made in essentially the form they appear to us now. Species do not originate from one another, but are discretely created groups. Man is a being who in his physical nature belongs entirely to the animal world: he shares in the nature of animals, his origin is the same, and the laws of his reproduction are similar. However, his essential *human* nature transcends his animal nature. Voegelin's most exact illustration of this archetype in its "pure" form can be found in his outline of the anthropology of Thomas à Kempis (*RI*, 1–3).

THE IMMANENT ARCHETYPE

THE PROCESS OF IMMANENTIZATION IN BIOLOGY

In his introduction to *Die Rassenidee in der Geistesgeschichte*, Voegelin listed four central conclusions that provide the context for the structure of his argument about the meaning of modern race-

---

11. Voegelin's summary of Herder's ideas (*RI*, 61) is reminiscent of the tone of the Old Testament book Ecclesiastes.

ideas and theory. The first "essential result" of the study was the discovery of the date at which the term "organism" was given its modern meaning (*RI*, 11). The second showed how the problem of infinity emerged as a transitory problem between the two archetypes of the natural world (*RI*, 12). The third was the "presentation of the transformation of the image" of species from separate, static, intransitive unities to "the idea of the development of species and their real derivation from one another" (*RI*, 12). The fourth, already implied, was the general discovery that the image of man was transformed in tandem with the image of life in general.

The great transformation of the archetype of life and the transformation of the images of the various phenomena within the archetype was from a transcendent to an immanent image of the whole and its parts. In accordance with the general structure of Voegelin's study, "the transition from the transcendent to the immanent perspective can be traced in every particular of the problem of life" (*RI*, 99). Voegelin began his examination of the transformation with the *Theoria Generationis* of C. F. Wolff, but Wolff was certainly not the first to begin rejecting the purely transcendental, mechanical construction of the epigenesists and pre-formationists. Georg E. Stahl, whom Wolff is said to have admired,[12] developed a theory of organism that anticipated the work of many later speculative biologists. Stahl argued that organism and mechanism were fundamentally unlike, so that the mechanical physiology of most of his colleagues was in error: "In the living organism, the soul is the essential part; the body exists for the sake of the soul and is controlled by the soul . . . it is always the soul which ultimately keeps the body together and keeps it from disintegrating."[13] Although Stahl imagined a soul that penetrates the material body, controlling and maintaining its process, as well as directing its voluntary motions, rather than one that resides in the body, with the body separately carrying out its physical, vital functions, the soul and the body nevertheless appeared to be separate entities that interpenetrate one another, but are not of the same essence.

Wolff, who has been considered one of the first "nature philosophers," took Stahl's speculation one step further. The notions of na-

12. Gasking, *Investigations into Generation*, 97.
13. This is Nordenskiold's summary, *History of Biology*, 181.

ture philosophy, a part of eighteenth-century Romanticism, were pantheistic.[14] The most important feature for our present study, however, is that, beginning with Wolff, the nature philosophers held that the vital force of living creatures was inherent in the creatures themselves. Growth was considered a basic phenomenon of the universe, requiring no further explanation, especially not in materialistic, nonanimate terms.[15] Voegelin found that although Wolff could not entirely remove himself from the segmentary construction, he held that a living entity was not a mechanism, but a "mechanical body, animated by the *vis motrix*," a "force that cannot be localized in a material component, and that is in a relationship of 'employment' with them" (*RI,* 88). According to Voegelin, the ideas presented by Wolff approach the idea of the pneumatic body that incorporates itself in material. Like Herder's, the speculations of Wolff come close to the "intellectual unitary form" construction type we outlined in the second chapter. In the end, the archetype represented by the segmentary construction retained its power over Wolff, but in his speculation, segmentation is no longer pure. Mechanism and animal would begin to flow into one another, becoming "the two sides of a single ontic element" (*RI,* 91).

Voegelin continued his analysis, examining now the theories of Leibniz and Oken. The end result of their formulations was that the organism was transformed from "a piece of material that is constructed according to a plan from without" into a "living substance that unfolds, regenerates and reproduces according to an inner law" (*RI,* 11). The path, which we need not trace here, was a tortuous matter of redefining the old concepts, and of reconceptualizing the old ideas, so that a new image of the living organism emerged.[16] The organic idea (Voegelin's term) replaced the duality of matter and soul. The organism became "a concrete, effective, final substance, that takes materials to itself, and in the act of its accretion, can, in accordance with its idea, transform them and reorganize them into members of itself" (*RI,* 98). In the new image of the living entity, Voegelin continued, the two aspects of Ray's essence (or Woltereck's norm of reaction) "melt together," so that the essential idea of the

14. Gasking, *Investigations into Generation,* 97, 149; Nordenskiold, *History of Biology,* 286–98.
15. Gasking, *Investigations into Generation,* 151.
16. See *RI,* 92–98.

individual, presented to the observer through the "complex of characteristics," and the "cause of the appearance of the image" become one (*RI,* 98).

The struggle to realize a new, immanent image repeated itself on the level of species. A reciprocal relationship developed between speculative theories of species and theories of the individual, because the individual is the "carrier," as it were, of the inherent lawful unfolding and replication of species. Voegelin divided the immanentization of species into two steps. In the first step, the Christian explanation so strongly accepted by Linnaeus was rejected, and the creative act of God that gives the lawful form of species a beginning was removed from a theory of species. Here we see the importance of Voegelin's second finding: if we remove the creative act of God from an explanation of the origin and order of species, we are left with explanations that leave us with an infinite regress of ascendants. Explaining a phenomenon in reality with an infinite series is absurd, so we may question the epigenetic and pre-formationist theories on the basis of that absurdity. The idea of infinity is a mathematical construct, but this "abstraction of reason" does not have a corresponding phenomenon in reality (*RI,* 102). An infinite series explains nothing, and means nothing. Therefore, replacing God with an infinite series was concluded with the suggestion that species could not be an infinite series of encapsulations, but that the law of formation carried in each individual was an immanent, finite law, inhering in the substance of life itself.

The failing of the speculations on infinity was that they were attempts to see a whole in the (infinite) hierarchy of individuals in a series. When the formative principle of a species became immanent, the alternative was to find the determining order of species in the "closed individual" (*RI,* 105). Voegelin outlined several attempts to symbolize the inner organizing principle of the organism. All were similar in intent and conception to the "organic idea." The organism became a primordial phenomenon, a holistic entity that carries the vital urge within itself, as a part of itself. The organism creates itself, renews itself, and maintains itself (*RI,* 110). Species then became the unifying idea given by the expression of the same immanent ordering principle residing in many organisms at once. The difference between the old view of the nature of the individual and species and the relationship of one to the other and the new is perhaps most succinctly illustrated in the fact that formerly the individual was explained as an exemplar emerging from the unity of the species; in the new image, species is explained as the formational, behavioral, and reproductive unity of a group of individuals. The exemplar of a species, carrying within itself all other exemplars, becomes the carrier of a formative urge that in its unfolding is the species itself.

The transformation of the images of species and individual also resulted in the transformation of the image of the natural world in general. From a static conception of species ranked alongside one another with boundaries that cannot be trespassed, the image changed to an unfolding natural world that we can speak of as having a history: "The transcendent idea of creation is replaced with the immanent idea of history" (*RI*, 114).

Voegelin found the process of transformation of this part of the archetype to be the most complex. We need not concern ourselves further with it here, except to note that in the immanent conception of the biosphere, all living forms are historically (and ontically) related to one another, and arise out of one another.[17] The continuity of life-forms is not based on a Kantian "regulative idea of reason," a transcendent continuity that is not part of the phenomena themselves, but rather, it is a "constitutive principle of the experience of nature," a "real part of natural phenomena themselves" (*RI*, 117–18).

An immanent conception of species and biosphere does not noticeably alter the method or epistemology of classification. Our comments on Ray and Willughby establish the parameters well enough for both archetypes: classification of organisms, though it is based on observation, is transcendent, since in immanentist theory, *all* organisms are related. If we desire to order the living world in a meaningful fashion, our transcendental categories will of necessity impose a certain rigidity on the lawfulness of the unfolding of species. Otherwise, our classes will flow into one another, and our classification will become meaningless (*RI*, 125–26).

THE IMMANENT IMAGE OF MAN

In a few brief strokes, we have sketched out the backdrop against which we can understand the modern ideas of individual, race, and mankind. The classical transcendent idea of man can be illustrated

17. For details of the transformation, see *RI*, 113ff.

in Christian anthropology. Man is a being separate from the rest of the natural world. The meaning of his existence is not completed in this world, but extends into a realm beyond the grave. The measure of this earthly life is transcendent, not only in its extension beyond death, but also in the daily activities of individuals, and in the order of community that is established here. In some schools of Christian thought, the political community represents and emulates a transcendent order that reaches into the activities and self-interpretations of each of its members.

The transcendent idea of man first loses its force from the side of biological investigations of man, but an anthropology that "wants to consider man as an intellectual unitary being" must analytically reconcile itself to the immanent image of life if it is to give a persuasive account of man's nature once the immanent biological explanations have been accepted as truthful. Life has become an immanent, primal phenomenon; because it is an integral part of human being, it becomes difficult to picture the human mind as having a transcendent source of existence, or of being the locus of such a source, when the vital impetus of all life is inherent in the life-form itself. On the basis of immanentist biology, human life and being becomes a primal phenomenon in all its aspects in the same manner as animal life. The impetus to rid speculative activity of the various segmentary and epiphenomenal constructions of man, and to view his existence as wholly immanent, locked in itself, came from the conceptual and empirical success of this endeavor on the level of the other, nonhuman phenomena of life (*RI*, 128).

In immanentizing human existence, we replace the dualism of mind, soul, and reason, or spirit and body, with the "concept of the human person as a unified, unbroken entity, that is neither body-less and psychic, nor psyche-less and physical in nature." As on the level of the organism, wrote Voegelin, the "schema of the division between matter and mind must be laboriously overcome in order to make it possible to imagine the indivisible unity of the manner of existence that is sought" (*RI*, 128).

The three thematic aspects of Voegelin's account at the level of man are made most visible within the problem of death. In the older, transcendent archetypes of life, the image of human life was not finite, but eternal. Human life did not end here, but the final salvation from worldly troubles and cares was realized in an existence beyond the grave. Consequently, hope, aspiration, and human effort

98

were directed not only to the matters of this world, but to matters beyond. The essence of human life (mind, soul, or spirit) did not originate in this world, and did not remain or end in it.

Death is a limit. It is a limit to knowledge; faith and hope, not knowledge, bear us across the boundary of the limit. Most importantly, death is a limit to human activity. The world, all the artifacts and activities of men, existed before any one individual, and it will continue to exist after that individual has died. The question of meaning arises in this particular case, I believe, because it is in the nature of the human mind to be able imaginatively to extend itself beyond its temporal boundaries. Our observation that the world, what we build in it, and the consequences of what we do in it, will remain after us makes the extinction of death abhorrent to the extending mind. We begin to wonder what the abhorrence means. Voegelin later used the symbol of tension to express the gap between our finite existence and our experience of eternity.[18] Interpretations and discourses about death are attempts, partially successful, to resolve the tension. Death as a limit produces its own culture and its own discourses that impute meaning to experience of it.

The idea of human species, like all ideas of other species, was cast in the form of a series. Accompanying this idea was the idea of forward motion, a succession of generations headed toward a goal. Where a *telos* of the group is a speculative problem (again engendered by a quest for meaning), the relationship of the individual to the group becomes a concomitant question. These two separate but related problems occur in both transcendent and immanent speculations. Transcendentally, the problem may be solved by separating the perfectibility of individual life from the perfectibility of the group, by rejecting the possibility of the perfectibility of the group, or by speculating that the contribution of each individual furthers the historical perfection of the group, while individual (spiritual) perfection continues beyond mundane human existence.[19]

18. I know of a no more succinct expression of this tension than in Koheleth's reflection in Ecclesiastes, "He has placed eternity in our hearts." The heart, a finite faculty of human emotion and will, located in the body, contains within itself the eternal. We are given here an exquisite image of the mortal-eternal tension that is in every person, displaying itself in a variety of responses to it.

19. Voegelin's discussion of Lessing's and Kant's speculation on the topic (*RI*, 128–34), provides examples of constructions that reject the perfectibility of the group and of constructions that speak in terms of mundane contribution and supra-

In an immanentist explanation of meaning in a life that proceeds toward death, we may likewise separate the life of the individual from that of the group, or we may reject the possibility of the qualitative betterment of the life of the group, or we may link the life of the individual with the improvement of the group. However, since there are no transcendent standards, we may reject the possibilities of perfectibility or any qualitative improvement at all in the existence of either group or individual. To answer the latter objection to the meaningfulness of ideals first, we may note that a sense of striving, achievement, and "movement towards" seems to be an integral part of human existence. While this does not imply that perfection is possible, it certainly implies that human existence is inexplicably impoverished if life remains without goals and ideals. Impoverished life is not impossible—indeed, it may be a prevalent form of human existence—but it is nevertheless less than what is possible. To some individuals, seeking less than the best, or at least the possible, is to succumb to less than human life. Striving and idealization cannot be justified beyond themselves; they are for their own sake, and they are integral to human life.

For those who seriously engage in a life directed toward the best, the relationship of group and individual may become problematic. If we assume the first possibility, that the individual can be separated from the group, we encounter several difficulties. The most important of these is that a man is part of a community, at least insofar as his knowledge of the world and his language stem not only from his own experience, but from his intercourse with other men. Therefore, it is impossible to separate cleanly individual and community. Second, achievement and the recognition resulting from it are respectively measured and bestowed by a community of men. In addition to the political terms in which we may cast the problem, it is clear that, similarly to all other living entities, man is embedded in a group because he is born. This connection to at least two other members of the human species, who in turn are members of an unending line of ascendants, is enough to indicate that the problem is of some consequence. The further intricacies of the problem of the relationship between individual, community, and the world that men build and live in together, are beyond the scope of the present essay. It is enough

---

mundane perfection. Kant also attempted a construction separating the perfectibility of group and individual, but Voegelin considered it to be unsuccessful (*RI,* 133).

to recognize that the intimate relationship between individual and group is of such strength that those making immanentist speculations concerning man assumed, apparently without question, that the fact of the connection constituted a problem requiring consideration.

It is not necessary to separate group and individual radically in order to maintain the separate integrity of both. It is clear from Voegelin's comments on Lessing that the group may be seen to remain relatively static in its realization of an idea, and that the individuals alone may grow toward whatever the ideal is considered to be, thereby coincidentally bringing the group closer to the goal of perfection. The emphasis is on the side of the individual; the betterment or progress of the group is an epiphenomenon of individual achievement. However, if we take the possibility of an ultimate *telos* of the group seriously, then it is difficult to escape a sense of alienation from an objective that cannot be realized in one's personal existence, but that one contributes toward realizing.

Voegelin used Kant's well-known examination of the possibilities of the perfection of the individual and of mankind to illustrate the essential problems with which all immanentist theories of the individual and mankind would have to grapple. According to Voegelin, Kant uncovered an alienation in immanent existence between *telos* and individual, regardless of whether the *telos* was of the individual or of the group. The perfection of man is impossible in a finite existence alone. Reason and sensuality could not, in Kant's estimation, be reconciled.[20] This principle may be expanded; any ideal that is completely nonsensual in nature will come into conflict with sensuality. The principle is implied in Voegelin's comparison of Kant's solution to the problem with that of Augustine. In both cases, the "incomprehensible corruption of being in time . . . becomes whole and well again in the eternity of God" (*RI,* 133). If immanent perfection of man is impossible, then it is necessary to postulate an immortal soul if we are not to become alienated from our own existence because of the split between the goal of life and the impossibility of attaining it in this life (*RI,* 131). If the *telos* of human life is not attainable in this life, then mundane human existence becomes meaningless, a striving and yearning for nothing.

Similarly, if we attribute the possibility of perfection in terms of

---

20. *RI,* 132. For Kant's discussion, see Immanuel Kant, *Critique of Practical Reason,* trans. Lewis White Beck (New York, 1985), 114–39.

an ideal to the human species as a whole, relegating its realization to a distant future, and consider the present generation as a step in ascension to the goal, the meaning of the present individual's life is to work for the good of a future generation. Once again, the split between the possibility of realizing the goal of one's efforts and the goal itself alienates a man from his own, now seemingly futile, life: "Through his efforts, the individual becomes the means to an end, the perfected life of the last generations."[21] Voegelin perceived an element of the mathematical conception of a series in Kant's speculation at this point. The individual is an "element in a series . . . in which the meaning of life appears as an accidental, alienating question, disturbing the tidy construction" (RI, 130). The problem of infinite series arose for Kant in this connection for the same reason that Voegelin considered his thought to be the first step in the immanentization of human existence: both rejected the plausibility of an ultimate perfection of man through a direct act of God (RI, 4). Kant's rejection of a divine act was the original source of his alienation, because the fulfilment of telos became an eternal process rather than a gift of grace. "Pure practical reason" dictated that the individual would eternally progress in a spiritual state toward perfection (RI, 131–32). This point is important, because it means that the transformation of the archetype is not merely a matter of "changing one's mind" about what one sees, but may begin with the rejection of the foundation of the old archetype, in this case a personal, acting, but transcendent God. Whatever the philosophical objections to such a conception of God may be, the point is that the source of transcendence must be slowly transformed, especially in its relationship to the phenomena of the archetype, before there is a plausible need for an archetypical transformation.

If we closely follow Voegelin's analysis, it appears that he found in Kant's arguments three specific difficulties that immanentist theories of human existence had to overcome. First, individual reason and the reason of the species had the same structure. Consequently, the "totality" of individual life and the "totality" of the life of the group could not be separated from one another to make their differences clear (RI, 135). Second, Kant's idea of mankind was egalitarian in the sense that all men moved together toward their goal. Kant

21. RI, 135; cf. RS, 142–43.

could not conceive of a qualitative difference between the roles of individuals in humanity's realization of its *telos,* so that he was unable to conceive of leaders who, because of their superior realization of reason, could lead the rest more closely and quickly toward the ultimate, universal perfection in reason (*RI,* 138–39). Third, reason, the ideal standard of both the individual and mankind, was transcendent, so that it of necessity had to stand in opposition to the immanent, sensual nature of human being. To overcome the split would be impossible unless reason also became an immanent idea. Reason could no longer be a kind of transcendental perfection, but it would have to become an immanent quality of man that, together with his sensuality, formed a whole (*RI,* 143).

THE IMAGE OF THE COMPLETE MAN

The three difficulties that arose in the period of transition from the transcendentalist to the immanentist archetypes of human existence, and that were illustrated in the arguments of Kant, were answered in immanentist speculation by the image of the "complete man" (*RI,* 141). Again, the fully developed image did not arise instantaneously, but was the product of a lengthy development. The embodiment of the image in all its stages of development was Goethe (*RI,* 140, 144, 149).

The image of the "complete man" and the "demonic nature" began with the experience of the competitive, laissez-faire state and its concomitant phenomena of specialization through the division of labor. The specialization of the individual, which could be considered a fragmentation of the whole person, meant that not one could realize his full humanity (*RI,* 136). The competition from which a social unity seemed nevertheless to arise showed that the totality of the individual and the totality of mankind did not necessarily have to be of the same nature. In contradiction to Kant, it was possible for an idea to emerge that all men are neither the same nor equal in their abilities nor in their contribution to the betterment of mankind. Consequently, when Schiller attempted to reestablish the unity of the individual in the face of his fragmentation in an age of specialization, he did not need to include all mankind in his quest, but he could speculate that a small group of select individuals, unequally gifted in comparison to the rest, might be the vanguard of a general improvement in the fragmented condition of mankind. In the person of

Goethe, Schiller found an individual who had overcome the trends of specialization and compartmentalization, thereby embodying the ideal of the total person, an image arising from the idea of the well-rounded man of antiquity (*RI*, 136, 141). By making qualitative distinctions between the "complete man" and the rest of the population, Schiller introduced the beginning of a division within the group that had formerly been considered an egalitarian unity in the Kantian system. A "select group," or elite, whose collective and individual life was qualitatively distinct from the mundane existence of the mass, emerged.

Schiller also took the first step in overcoming the third difficulty raised in Kant's philosophizing, the transcendence of the ideal. The complete man was the embodiment of the unity of sensuality and reason, so that neither alone could be said to represent the nature of man; reason was an immanent quality of the demonic man. The life of the complete man was the "beautiful life," and the community that such demonic men would build was an "aesthetic" community, immanently realizable in the present (*RI*, 141, 144). With the introduction of the idea of the "aesthetic state" that could be established on the characteristics of an elite of representatives of the "beautiful life," the "strength of an idea of the incremental continual progress of humanity to an endlessly distant goal was broken" (*RI*, 145). The community of the elite was a present, actually existing image, which could serve as the standard of excellence and which would be the embodiment of immanent perfection for the community.

From these three starting points, Voegelin showed how the problem of infinity, which we have expressed on the human level in terms of the problem of mortality, was gradually overcome in the new image of man. The new image is one of an individual, singular, intellectual force, that begins new things, and that is without precedent or connection to previous events: "The appearance of the intellectual force of man is sudden, not bound to progress, nor does it unequivocally bring it about; its origin is inexplicable, and its effects incalculable" (*RI*, 145). The workings of the intellectual force are not connected to the group in such a way that we could discover a direction of progress; "indeed, a progress is noticeable in events, but it is not a progress hastening toward a goal, but one that can only be adequately described in organic analogies" (*RI*, 145). "Enjoyment of life," "happiness and activity," and "enjoyment of existence" are phrases used to describe the only possible "purpose" that life may have. "The individual is no longer an element in a series analogous to mathematics," but "the nature of man is given in an inner perception in which the structure of the nature of existence appears as the structure of the meaning of existence" (*RI*, 147). The immanent disposition (*Gemüt*) finds the meaning of existence in its own existence, knowing that its singular existence may be connected to further meanings, but that these are a mystery that cannot be speculatively united into a whole. The striving and longing of individual existence cannot be the reliable source of a speculation about the meaning of the existence of the group. The meaning of singular existence, its yearning and its self-development, are speculatively separated from the life of the group, and its meaning is found in its self-development alone (*RI*, 148).

At the same time that a *telos* of the group is rejected as a source of meaning, the body and mind of the individual are unified in such a way that a psychophysical conception equivalent to the concept of the nonhuman organism emerges. The bodily faculties flow into the "spiritual, intellectual, and psychic traits," so that they are mutually dependent for their full realization in the life of the individual (*RI*, 148). Voegelin found that the idea of human individuality, the self-contained unitary being, was completed in the theories of Carus. The idea of the well-born, eugenic man becomes the final symbol of the immanent human being. There is a substantial group of symbols that surrounds this idea, but we may leave them, and consider the most important one of them for our purpose, the idea of the totality of the individual entity. The new human being is an entity that is neither body nor mind, but both at once. Conforming to the construction type that Voegelin called the "intellectual unitary form" construction, body and soul (or mind) are united, the emphasis being on the psychic element, so that the body becomes the field of expression of the soul. A defective body will hinder the self-expression and self-development of the soul, so that the two are intimately bound into a single entity in Carus' conception (*RI*, 154). The life of the body and of the mind are intimately linked. Consequently, there must be a connection between psychic existence and the wider aspects of physical existence. The problems of biological speculation in the human sphere become important for consideration of the nature of human mind. We can no longer split them as was possible in

105

transcendentalist accounts of the nature of man. The relationship between individual and species becomes a particularly interesting problem since we have seen that Kant's feeling of alienation, because of the finitude of the individual and the infinitude of the progressing series in which the individual is embedded, was overcome by eliminating the possibility of discovering teleological meaning in the progression of the group, or of imputing meaning to a progress of the individual. An immanentist quest for excellence is not a progress, but an "aesthetic life," a living of life to the fullest.

The well-born individual is a member of a larger group, most of whose members we must assume are not well born, and do not achieve the full expression of their psychophysical being. The reply to this observation, which Voegelin summarized, is not an explanation, but nothing more than an observation itself: "differences belong to the nature of humanity and its unfolding" (*RI*, 153). With this simple reply, we have made possible the transition from a discussion of individuality to a consideration of the group, the particular race. Mankind is not an "aggregate of innumerable minds of equal condition and ability . . . but an organic whole, that is not composed of the same elements, but from various kinds [of elements]" (*RI*, 153). This insight permits us to speak of particularly gifted individuals, the well-born few, and it may also permit us to differentiate between groups on the basis of conglomerations of conditions, traits, and abilities.

RACE THEORY

There are two categories of theories of race. The first comprises those theories that are speculative solutions to problems concerning the ontic nature of man and his membership in a biological series that extends into the psychic realm. The second category includes those speculations concerned with the relationship of the various distinct groups of biological series in the unfolding of history. The latter theories imply the assumption that the former are a meaningful way of talking about human beings. At the same time, the former are based on a primal manner of seeing that is closely associated with the political and historical explanations of the latter. I will call the first category psychophysical theories of race, and the second category political theories of race. Voegelin closely examined the race theories of H. F. K. Guenther, Lenz, Othmar Spann,

Walter Scheidt, and Eugen Fischer. They contain several common themes, which I will present here, that show, first, how most modern race theories are philosophically inadequate and, second, the importance of the immanent archetype to their formation.

Psychophysical theories are hindered by a basic problem whose explication and repetition, as we have already seen, runs like a thread through both of Voegelin's books: "that man is a psychophysical unity can be as little disputed as the possibility that the body may be studied in isolation with natural-scientific methods—but how these two facts are to be reconciled with one another, and how the nature of man is to be determined, remains an unmastered problem" (*RI, 44*). Nearly everything that we could say about psychophysical theories of race has already been anticipated in the first three chapters of the present essay. Race theories are essentially speculative constructions regarding the nature of man that represent attempts to explain the psychophysical unity of man in such a way that it is possible to make consistent and coherent statements about the visible behavioral and morphological unity of particular groups of individuals. Consequently, "the problem of race is a part of the body-soul problem" (*RS, 8*). The arguments of Voegelin's anthropology may be brought to bear with full force on the theoretical constructions of race theory.

The beginning of race theory is in the biological study of species, but it never remains within the boundaries established by such a study. The agenda of all race theorists includes the examination of not only the physical, but also the psychic characters of what are called races. On the basis of this agenda, race theorists may encounter one or more of a number of theoretical problems. The first and most obvious of these has been discussed enough that it can be mentioned here without extensive comment; race theories that attempt systematically to explain the nature of man in terms of one or more laws that govern the appearance and development of that nature generally do so on the basis of speculative construction rather than theoretical analysis. Consequently, they contradict Voegelin's premises for a good philosophical anthropology, and are open to the criticisms we have outlined in Chapter Two.

Race theorists insist on transgressing the boundary between body and mind because they are well aware that a community is based essentially on the mind, not the body. The ideas of a community of men reside in and inform their minds, so that the images and focal ideas of a community, which guide the behavior and actions of its members, are an essential element in understanding the general form of a community or a racial group. The error of race theorists is to suppose that vaguely defined mental and physical elements are all determined by the same biological and/or geographical factors, so that a study of the body will yield insights into the nature of the mind.

The remainder of the problems originate in most race theorists' tendency to ignore epistemological questions associated with the body-soul problem. Theories of race begin with the biological observation that there is a continuity of physical traits and characteristics from ascendant to descendant in a reproductive series. The central focus of Voegelin's critical analysis of race theories was the insistence of race theorists that the results of a "legitimate scientific undertaking" in the sphere of biology and physical anthropology, namely, categorizing groups according to morphological characteristics, could be "in some manner scientifically relevant for mental matters" (*RS*, 35). On the basis of Voegelin's ontology, this premise was unacceptable. It is important to remember that the *immanent* idea of the nature of life, in which race theorists participate, does not imply that the ontic unity of man is equivalent to an ontological singularity. In other words, ontologically distinct aspects of being, even if they occur in unity with one another, must nevertheless be treated with the epistemological methods appropriate to their respective natures. Voegelin's argument was that most race theorists ignored this fact.

The speculative union of body and mind in race theory is discussed in part on the basis of a Darwinian account of heredity. We have already seen the difficulties surrounding this argument in its biological form, but race theorists compound the problems by insisting that not only physical traits are "inherited," but mental traits as well. Two questions immediately arise: what is a "mental trait"? how is it transferred from parents to offspring? Neither question is adequately answered by theorists of race.

The first question concerning the nature of mental traits is not answered because it is impossible to do so on the basis of natural-scientific concepts and methods. The substance of the mind is inaccessible to phenomenal study. At the same time, it is clear that behavior, which is a phenomenon, may be studied by empirical science. However, behavior and trait are not equivalent (*RS*, 74). Behavior and other outer manifestations of mental characteristics are indicators of mental traits, but they are not the traits themselves. Traits must be treated as ideas that reside in the complex of phenomena that manifest them, but such a complex, to repeat, is not a possible object of phenomenal science.

Although mental traits and characteristics are not objects of natural science, they are objects of cognition, as are all ideas, so that the natural scientist, like anyone else, can recognize them and talk about them. However, he cannot measure or examine them "scientifically" (*RS*, 74, 79). Having perceived the mental traits of a manifold of individuals, we can establish categories of them, so that we may classify and distinguish groups of individuals on the basis of psychic traits and characteristics common to all of their particular members (*RS*, 85–86). This activity, however, is not an activity of a phenomenal science, because we are not treating phenomena, but substance. Voegelin noted that at the time the modern race theories were developed, the disciplines that would be needed to carry out the task of characterizing and classifying psychic types were either nonexistent or in their infancy. A theory of types could only be developed on the basis of an enormous quantity of work concerning the nature of the mind in its relationship to experienced reality (*RS*, 85). Most of the race theories that Voegelin examined did not contain even the beginnings of an endeavor to create an exact instrument for working out psychic types, but their authors were content with vague or simplistic categories of types whose inadequacy Voegelin easily demonstrated.[22]

In the next step of their agenda, the race theorists passed over these epistemological problems, and proposed that mental qualities (whose nature was never adequately determined) must somehow be connected to the general process of heredity in the same way that physical traits are. Thus, they also ignored the problems associated

---

22. *RS*, 86ff. Voegelin believed he had the first beginnings of such an instrument in his *Über die Form des amerikanischen Geistes*, where he used as his basis for a determination of intellectual types "the structure of speculation about time" (*RS*, 85). He also gave an example of the use of intelligence tests to indicate racial types, demonstrating in his analysis both the logical fallacies of the methods used and the inadequate procedures used to apply them (*RS*, 88–91).

with a theory of heredity, thereby encountering considerable difficulties in describing, let alone explaining, the process of inheriting
mental traits. Voegelin further pointed out that race theorists had a
habit of associating a psychic trait with every cultural and artistic
achievement. This habit stemmed from their misunderstanding that
not only the physical but also the mental world is an environment
in terms of which we must understand both the mental characteristics of individuals and groups, and their intellectual and spiritual
activities. Intellectual and spiritual traits are not directly accessible
to the natural sciences, nor can they be simply associated with faculties localizable in genetic material. The problems of environment
and individual that Voegelin cast in the form of the inner-outer
schema repeat themselves analogously in the realm of the human
mind. Dante and Beethoven, to use Voegelin's example, were not
simply "rather gifted fellows"; rather, the appearance of their genius must be understood within the context of their time in cultural
history, as well as within the contingencies of their own personal
lives (*RS*, 81). Furthermore, the particular artistic, technical, or hu-
manitarian achievements of an individual are based on a *series* of
faculties, of which not all may be mental; two individuals may be
equally successful in the same field, and yet widely different "faculties" could be the operative factors for their successes. Consequently, we cannot in a facile manner attach a particular talent to a
particular field of activity (*RS*, 83).

   None of what I have said so far is intended to imply that the continuity of traits from ascendant to descendant is a chimera. The idea
of heredity rests in "a series of basic experiences," including the
experience of sexual reproduction, the knowledge that in their form,
men are similar but also have variations from individual to individual within the boundaries of their similarity, and the observation that
children share certain mental and physical traits with their parents.
Second, man experiences himself as a whole, so that in an immanentist conception of his own nature, "it will always be a reasonable
claim that man as a whole is woven into the events of the line of
succession" (*RS*, 65). Consequently, it is not senseless to imagine
that all of the individual is embedded in the immanent series of ascendants and descendants.

   Even if we accept that intellectual and physical traits are "passed
on" as a unity and in the same mechanism, we have still not discov-

ered the answer to what this mechanism could be. Voegelin found the question left unanswered by most of the race theorists (*RS*, 85). He himself did not doubt the "connection between body, soul, and mind," nor that "the blood-inheritance is of greatest significance for the mental unitary being of man," but he was "just as convinced, that this significance can only be found through the most thorough study of the psychic structure itself" (*RS*, 87).

Under an immanent conception of life, the apparent unity of mind and body may be interpreted as a kind of fate of the individual. The "structure and unfolding of the individual person" appears to be predetermined in its entirety if it is based wholly on the transfer from parents to offspring of the vital element, whatever it may be, and wherever it may reside, that lawfully determines the being of the individual (*RS*, 65–66). We must stress this point, because it illuminates a fundamental inconsistency that seemed to govern the speculations contained in a number of race theories that Voegelin analyzed.

Fatality is a basic human experience whose coherence is supported by the same kinds of experiences that create the idea of heredity. Given both this experience and the prejudices of the natural sciences, it is easy to suppose that each individual's entire nature is a result of the lawful unfolding of an immanent vital principle that articulates the species of which he is a member. According to Voegelin, race theorists generally did not understand the logical consequences of such a supposition. If the operations of the mind are bound entirely to the body, then they are physical phenomena, masquerading as something else. If the mind is completely dependent on physical process (in reproduction) for its coming into being and its unfolding, then the body must also determine its workings on a broader scale. Voegelin argued that if we make mental and physical process and characteristics entirely and consistently parallel, then "it follows that we must posit a series of occurrences of the body running parallel to our entire experience of the mind, that clings intimately to the series of psychic experiences" (*RS*, 66). Every artistic and intellectual endeavor would have its physical condition, not only in the broad sense, but in every detail of mental and spiritual activity. The mind would become nearly an epiphenomenon of the body.

As we have already argued, this kind of construction contradicts another basic aspect of human existence, the experiences of freedom. The two varieties of logically opposed experiences are a part of the duality of human existence. Experiences of insight, inspiration, and willful activity run parallel to experiences of fate, handicap, and restriction. We have already argued that the experiences of the mind are unlike those of the body.[23] Voegelin maintained that experiences of freedom were not restricted to the mind, nor experiences of determination to the body, but that "our body is not only a passive field for impressions from the environment, but an active field of expressions and action" (RS, 68). The body extends into the world and acts within it. Similarly, the human mind is not only "the center and source of action and power," but also an "experiencing, receptive mind." The mind is "embedded in the intellectual communities at all levels." Nation, family, and intimate friends together constitute the environment and fate of the mind (RS, 68–69). Experiences of fate and freedom are the opposite poles of an aspect of the dualistic unity that is man.

Race theorists were happy to locate both physical and mental traits in the causal chain of reproduction, but "under the rubric of a tradition of acquired characteristics or of nurture," they separated out certain mental activities, placing them in an intended realm of freedom. Aside from the difficulties exposed by Voegelin's discussion of mind and body, the realm of freedom is not a natural-scientific postulate, but an idea arising from metaphysical speculation (RS, 71). As such, it arises from experiences, just as does the development of deterministic images of human existence, but it is not a conclusion from a natural-scientific investigation.

Voegelin did not consign all race theories to the same category of epistemological and ontological carelessness. He concluded the first part of Rasse und Staat with an analysis of two theories that he considered to be indicators of the direction in which a philosophically well-grounded theory of race should move. He concluded Die Rassenidee in der Geistesgeschichte with an outline of Carus' theory of race, written on the occasion of Goethe's 100th birthday.

23. "[A]n 'epistemology' that would explain to us that the mind is not that which it reveals of itself in immediate experience is not a completion of our knowledge, but a gathering of false judgements, contradicting our every-day experience of the mind" (RS, 67).

Voegelin found in Carus' theory "the first system of a division of races in which the unity of all apparent races is to be deduced more or less from particular analogous divisions of elemental phenomena" (*RI*, 155). Carus' theory was based on an immanentist image of man. The typology and classification of race was not based on physical characteristics alone, but on the unitary psychophysical complex that was manifested in the individual members of the group. The characteristics of the mind are not derived from, or dependent on, the characteristics of the body, but mind and body form a unit. The body is the field of expression of the mind, so that psychic characteristics begin to encompass the physical ones (*RI*, 155). The body does not, however, become an epiphenomenon of mind, but retains its ontological integrity.

In Carus' system, the races could be ranked according to their proximity to a norm, based on the nature of mind, that did not establish one race as normal and regard the others as deviations from the norm, but that was based on the idea of the complete man (*RI*, 157). Since, as we saw earlier, inequality of organisms is accepted as a basic condition of immanent life, it follows that some races would more closely approximate the norm than others. The well-born, completed, demonic man (Goethe), would arise from that race which, as a whole, "most completely fulfills the meaning of humanity" (*RI*, 158). Voegelin perceived the germ of the mythos of the Nordic man to be emerging from the works of Carus.

The theories of Ludwig Clauss and Othmar Spann, examined at the end of Voegelin's discussion of the systematic content of race theory, had two common themes that were, for Voegelin, the center of their usefulness as signposts toward a consistent and defensible immanentist theory of race.

First, both theorists seemed to take into account the ontological and epistemological problems of a theory of race. Neither displayed a facile desire to associate typologies of mind with simple physical characteristics, nor to make mind dependent on body. Both were aware of the unitary duality of human being, and developed their theories accordingly (*RS*, 102, 114). Second, their awareness of the psychological problems led them to invent symbols similar in content and intent to the "norm of reaction" or the "essence" to describe man's organic and psychic nature. In both theories, race is treated as an idea of formation, an expression of the phenomenal unity of a group of men. In Clauss, the idea of race, similarly to the norm of reaction, is "like a plan, according to which this individual is made, and that he now (perhaps imperfectly) embodies," at the same time that it is an idea of formation that "separates itself into many people and permeates their personal habitus." [24] Clauss in particular was not interested in establishing racial mental types on the basis of a few more or less defined "traits," but in accordance with Voegelin's own arguments, on the basis of an examination of the "structure of existence and the position of the 'I' in it" (RS, 100). The basis of an immanentist psychic typology is the attitude of a group of individuals toward the full span of existential experience.

I would add here that Voegelin, though he did not explicitly defend a position of his own, did not appear to be persuaded by the immanentist view of life, nor by the plausibility of a meaningful description of mankind in terms of racial divisions. His approval of the directions Spann's and Clauss's theories were taking was immanent to the project of developing a race theory in general. Despite numerous criticisms leveled at them, he argued that these two theories of race at least addressed the philosophical issues involved in the endeavor, and attempted to overcome the scientistic dogmas of other race theories, so that a science of race might develop from them. Consequently, the kinds of things that would be said by them concerning the nature of man would likely be of a different character than the scientistic theories of some that represented attempts to merge science with political and historical explanation.

24. L. W. Clauss, *Von Seele und Antlitz der Rassen und Völker* (Munich, 1929), 59, in *RS*, 93; *RS*, 94.

FIVE

Community and Idea

According to the ancients, according to Voegelin, "the quality of a society depends on the degree to which the life of reason . . . becomes a creative force in that society."[1] Some political ideas that inform the intellectual and spiritual life of a society conform more closely to the order discovered by reason than do others. Therefore, we can judge the relative quality of the content of ideas in terms of standards based on our rational theoretical and practical understandings of reality. In this way, Voegelin divided the "ethical and metaphysical" substance of ideas from their "correctness as a picture of social reality."[2] We argued in Chapter Two that ideas are forces that both shape and describe social reality, and in the following chapters we presented Voegelin's description and analysis of the presuppositions, contents, and form of race theory.

Ideologies of race were the intellectual formations that symbolically constituted at least one totalitarian regime in this century, Nazi Germany. Let us agree that the character of a community of men is in part based on the ideas that inform it; it then seems reasonable to ask if there is anything inherent in the form or content of the race-ideas we have discussed that would lend itself to implementation in a totalitarian regime. To answer this question properly, we must take a series of analytical steps. First, we will consider the question of the relationship between community and narrative. Sec-

1. Eric Voegelin, "Industrial Society in Search of Reason," in R. Aron (ed.), *World Technology and Human Destiny* (Ann Arbor, 1963), 34.
2. Voegelin, "Growth of the Race Idea," 34.

ond, we will compare narrative with modern race theories and indicate at least some of the ways in which the former differ from the latter. Third, we will turn to a summary of the relationship between race theory, ideology, and totalitarianism. We can then return to the question of the direct connections between race-ideas and totalitarianism, based on a comparison of narrative and ideological means of linking and expressing ideas.

The problem of narrative is important for an understanding of the totalitarian link with modern racism and race-ideas because a transformation of body symbols from one type to another is not in itself sufficient for destructive ideologies. Neither is a shift from one archetype of life or mankind or the biosphere to another. The additional component of a transformation of the kinds of stories we tell (in which our ideas are embedded) is required. In the fourth chapter, we traced Voegelin's analysis of the immanentization of biological concepts of descent and ascent, concepts that we laid out in detail in Chapter Three. Immanentization at the level of *communal* or political body ideas is important because it easily leads to the secularization of these ideas. Secularization, in turn, is important because the focus and meaning of human activity changes when God (or even "the gods") is no longer an actor in the account of that activity. Thus, the immanent archetype of race and the secularization of the community join to provide us with the new possibilities for archetypes of man and community. Here again we encounter the importance of understanding our example and its conceptual implications in the first chapter of the Egyptian poet.

In accordance with Voegelin's observation about the quality of ideas and its relationship to the quality of a society, we may note that neither the successful development nor the acceptance of any political symbol and the archetype of which it is a part appears to be necessarily influenced by that particular symbol's theoretical poverty or sophistication. Not all men are either rational or inclined to rational or even commonsense contemplation of the political ideas that inform their lives. Consequently, while it is sound, Voegelin's analysis probably serves only, unfortunately, as an understanding and censure of what actually came into existence, rather than as a prophylaxis for the actual emergence of political symbols themselves in his time, now, or in the future. Whatever their quality may be, in order for political symbols to be of significance, they must become a part of the political sphere. Voegelin traced the emergence of the race symbols in political reality fairly closely in the second half of *Rasse und Staat.*

Let us begin with the beginning of a story:

> Now these are the names of the sons of Israel who came to Egypt with Jacob; they came each one with his household: Reuben, Simeon, Levi and Judah; Issachar, Zebulun and Benjamin; Dan and Naphtali, Gad and Asher. And all the persons who came from the loins of Jacob were seventy in number, but Joseph was already in Egypt. And Joseph died, and all his brothers and all that generation. But the sons of Israel were fruitful and increased greatly, and multiplied, and became exceedingly mighty, so that the land was filled with them.
>
> Now a new king arose over Egypt, who did not know Joseph. And he said to his people, "Behold, the people of the sons of Israel are more and mightier than we. Come, let us deal wisely with them, lest they multiply and in the event of war, they also join themselves to those who hate us, and fight against us, and depart from the land." And so they appointed taskmasters over them to afflict them with hard labor.[3]

The story begins as a story of a community, not an individual.[4] The community's physical origins are in a single individual, Jacob. Yet from his loins the community expanded rapidly to seventy, and has now become an "exceedingly mighty" nation, filling the land. The vitality of the community, as a *community,* is emphasized five times within the last sentence of the first paragraph. The sons of Israel, the bearers of the communal story, are fruitful, prolific, and fill the land. The body-ideas of ascent, descent, generation, and biological relation that emerge in the context of the story are obvious.

Before delving into the numerous functions that the narrative serves for the community, let us consider one aspect of the archetype within which these readily recognizable body ideas are located. Jacob, too, has a father, whose name was Isaac, and his father was

3. Exodus 1:1–11a. This version was taken from the *New American Standard Bible* (New York, 1977).
4. The following analysis of narrative is drawn from Michael Goldberg, *Theology and Narrative: A Critical Introduction* (Nashville, 1982); Michael Goldberg, *Jews and Christians: Getting Our Stories Straight* (Nashville, 1985); Stanley Hauerwas, *The Peaceable Kingdom* (Notre Dame, Ind., 1983).

Abraham. Abraham, we are told in an earlier narrative that is linked to this one, made a covenant with God, initiated by God. It is as a result of this covenant that the narrative we are now examining takes place and, indeed, takes on its meaning for the covenantal community of Jacob (the descendant of Abraham), also called Israel, and his descendants, the "sons of Israel." Accordingly, the body-symbols employed here, though they do not have the mystical qualities of some of the Christian body-symbols we examined earlier, do have a transcendent reference, namely Jahweh, who covenants with his people (represented here by the symbol, "the sons of Israel"), and who is the central actor in the narrative that follows. The "sons of Israel" is yet another example of what Voegelin called "political ideas"; it does not refer to a strict biological fact, but serves as the symbolical element that binds together a community, in this case under a covenant with Jahweh.

We cannot engage here in an extended discussion of the Israelite archetype under which these particular body-symbols helped to make sense of the world.[5] As we examine the narrative by which these ideas were expressed and born, however, we will bring into focus those elements that most clearly distinguish it from modern race theory. The most important of these is the idea of divine covenant and its corollary, direct divine intervention in human affairs. Another is the idea of the individual embedded in a community tradition and in a line of ancestors and descendants, but responsible nevertheless for his or her own actions before God and before others of the community.

Out of the first paragraph of our sample passage, a number of story functions emerge. First, from "this . . . story's vantage point, the key for understanding the meaning of human experience is in the aggregate experience of a whole human community and not in the individual experiences of some random human being."[6] But second, the story also identifies itself with a human particularity, the "sons of Israel," who are its bearers. It is these individuals, brought together into a community, not voluntarily, but by birth, under a body-idea of biological descent and consequent commonality, whom

5. *OH* I is perhaps as good a description of the Israelite archetype as any available, though it contains no intensive discussion of body-symbols as such.
6. Goldberg, *Jews and Christians*, 26.

118

this story places in a particular locality with a particular history. It is *not* a story about just anyone, a paradigmatic myth. It claims to be a story about a particular group, the sons of Israel.

Further, in so doing the story locates its subjects, who are also its bearers, in space and time. Jacob is the man who has twelve sons, who are connected to a particular place and time. To get the details, we must turn to an earlier story, the knowledge of which this story presumes. But even apart from such a preceding narrative, insofar as Jacob and his twelve sons and the rest of the seventy from his loins are presumed to be historical individuals, it is clear that the story assumes a location in space and time for the events it recounts. The immediate place is Egypt, but when we refer to the preceding narrative, we discover that there is a more distant and compelling location in the background of this story, the land promised to Jacob and his fathers by God. And it is this land, this location, that is again brought to the forefront as the narrative continues beyond the present introduction.

Time has two elements in this narrative. The first is the wider context of this more particular story, namely the coming into being and passing away of successive generations. Jacob has died and so, indeed, have Joseph and the seventy of his generation. The increase over generation, the continual multiplication of this vital community has "filled the land" with its members. The second element of time is more particularistic. A new king arises over Egypt, one who, for reasons not given, is detached from the preceding story and the obligations this story seemingly imposed on his predecessors' behavior. And the new Pharaoh acts "now," beginning a new episode in the narrative.

The new Pharaoh's first act, a speech, further distinguishes the community that both suffers and bears this present narrative. "His people," the people whom Pharaoh claims to represent, are now distinguished from "them." The world is divided into distinct political spheres, and with this distinction come violence and suffering, mastery and slavery. For the individual, participation in the "we–them" is not voluntary, but mandatory. Once the lines have been drawn and the distinctions made, each community, perhaps already defined by differences in language, customs, dress, and sociopolitical organization, begins to play a different role in the story, and its members are inserted into the story willy-nilly as participants in it. Although

119

there may be some choice about where and how one will take part in the unfolding narrative, there can be no "objective" or "neutral" position: all individuals become a constituent part of what takes place.

The two different communities may tell different stories of the same event. By bearing those stories each community finds the context for self-understanding, both of members individually, and of itself as a whole. It is perhaps this final aspect of narrative that is most important for our purposes and also the most difficult characteristic to understand. This narration account, and others like it, provide us with a basis for answering the fundamental questions concerning human existence, including: Who am I? What is the world like? How should I behave? or even, Who is God?

The importance to us of narrative is that it is a familiar method of integrating various ideas into a whole, including the political community-ideas that bind together a community existing under a particular archetype. A narrative does not integrate such ideas in the first instance by means of dogmatic assertions, nor by means of philosophical analysis, nor even prima facie by means of presenting the entirety of an archetype, but simply through the narration itself, through the recounting of human acts and events and their context. Paradigmatic ideas, as we have described them, are one of the constituents of such a narrative. While a recounting of events establishes a context for self-understanding, it is only through the medium of various body, communal, and other political ideas, through the medium of analytical unities in diversity, that a story makes sense. Narratives bear and interconnect, in a coherent fashion, the ideas and symbols that shape a community. There is a reciprocal relationship, however, between ideas and the narratives that bear them. Some kinds of ideas do not permit a narrative medium as readily as others. Consequently, the means by which they can be and are integrated are of a different character than narratives such as the one just considered. For this reason, the narrative presentation of political community-ideas provides a unique contrast to the presentation of equivalent ideas by the race theories analyzed by Voegelin.

Like the Jewish community, the Christian community, too, is initially formed by and around a narrative that it bears and that in turn shapes its bearer. This narrative is the Gospel concerning Jesus

120

Christ.[7] Secondarily, this narrative account includes the history of the early Church, known as the Acts of the Apostles, and attributed to Luke, to whom the Third Gospel is also attributed. Finally, we may more distantly include in this literary corpus the largely non-narrative, expository, and exhortatory epistles of Paul and others to early church communities in the Roman Empire.

By answering the question "Who is Jesus?" the early Christian narrative also helps to answer the questions "Who am I?" "What must I do?" and "What is the world like?" The Gospel narratives, then, serve as the foundation of a community of believers that hear the story and accept it as an authoritative account of God's acting into history through the man, Jesus;[8] consequently, they accept it also as indicating authoritatively what it means to be a disciple of Jesus and accordingly how one should behave. Let us be reminded that a major component of the narrative's formative power is found in the symbols and ideas of community that it contains, including, for example, the idea of the "mystical body of Christ" and "the priesthood of all believers."

For the first three hundred years or so after the birth of Jesus, this account of God's decisive incursion into human history held a minority position in the wider Roman ecumene. It did not appear to be intended to serve as the central narrative, shaping the symbolic self-understanding of an imperial ecumene; and, indeed, it did not serve in such a capacity.[9] Nevertheless, in time Christians became numerous enough and politically influential enough that the archetypes, symbols, and ideas of the particularistic Christian community were transferred, sometimes forcefully (and never with the unanimous consent of all who called themselves Christians) into the wider, imperial political realm. Here they were now supposed to symbolize

7. I am aware of the numerous critical problems surrounding the early compilation of what we now know as the Four Gospels of the Christian writings. Narratives, however, can be maintained and transmitted in oral as well as written form. Consequently, the problems of redaction, source, form, and other kinds of criticism associated with the contemporary study of the early Christian writings do not impinge directly on the argument I am making here, nor, given my purpose for them, do they weaken our narrative examples.

8. For this appellation, see 1 Tim. 2:5.

9. For a further elaboration of this historical point, see Voegelin, *New Science*, 100–10, and John Howard Yoder, "The Constantinian Sources of Western Social Ethics" in Yoder, *The Priestly Kingdom* (Notre Dame, Ind., 1984), 135–47.

Christian existential truths through the medium of political structures and actions, rather than through the organization of the community of Christian believers and the actions of its members. Although the transfer of Christian theological truths and symbols was not always successful and, indeed, continues to be criticized by at least one long-standing tradition of Christian understanding, the transfer was successful enough that substantial portions of Christian community ideas informed the political self-understanding of Europe from roughly the time of Augustine to the end of the Middle Ages.[10] The central symbol of concern for our analysis is the Christian image of the body of Christ.

THE TRANSFORMATION OF CHRISTIAN BODY-IDEAS

Let us recall that "the idea of the bodily community is always a 'mythical' idea, [that] . . . establishes a *corpus mysticum.*" Body-ideas may claim the authoritativeness of science as their basis, but because of their political nature, they are never genuine scientific judgments about reality (*RS,* 14). Rather, they are symbols of experience and intent at the same time, residing in the human mind, where they maintain their emotive and formative power.

When Voegelin traced the transformation of body-ideas, especially from the image of the mystical body of Christ to the particularized, immanent ideas of the nation, he was careful to note that the nation, as a symbol, is not an "objective" concept, but a political idea with mystical and emotive components. Indeed, the idea of the nation has little or none of the ideas of the family or bloodlines remaining, but is based almost entirely on spiritual and intellectual symbols of physical unity. A nation is united by its culture, language, and ideas, rather than by bodily descent.[11]

The body of Christ is a symbol of the mystical unity of all like-minded believers who by faith and belief participate in the *pneuma* of Christ. The fullness of Christ's *pneuma* is spread over the membership of His body, of which He is the head; each member has his/her function in the body, so that the covering *pneuma* is diversified in the abilities and tasks of the members. The symbol is suffi-

10. See Yoder, "Constantinian Sources," and Yoder, "The Kingdom as Social Ethic," in *Priestly Kingdom,* 80–101; Voegelin, *New Science,* 106.
11. Voegelin, "Growth of the Race Idea," 294.

ciently elastic that it may be used to represent the unity of an entire continent of diverse peoples. Voegelin found three historical factors that were largely responsible for the transformation of the mystical body of Christ into the modern nation-state. In this context, it is important to keep in mind that the universal symbol of the Christian body did not have a monopoly in the field of body-ideas. Running parallel and competing with it were other ideas in which Voegelin found the seeds of an archetype and its ideas and symbols that could form a milieu within which race-ideas could eventually become credible.

First, the dynastic ideas of bloodlines challenged the Christian idea of *charisma* as the "determining factor of rulership." In the practical division of the body into its diverse members, those who led ostensibly did so on the basis of their charisma, their "gift" of leadership. The opposing principle of bloodlines made rulership an inherited office. Ability to rule and right to rule were more nearly united in the first instance than in the second, but in the second idea, actual bodily experiences of reproduction and continuity were more nearly employed as the motivating factors of a political symbol and a political system.[12]

The gradual secularization of Western Europe, beginning in the Renaissance (or perhaps the High Middle Ages) is well known. According to Voegelin, its origin lies in the community's loss of a sense of its own spiritual ideas to the point where their Christian meaning became lost. Reason, at first transcendent, but later an immanent idea, replaced the spirit of holiness of Christ; the unity of man and community became based on secular ideas. It was then possible to develop ideas less universal than the spirit of Christ, such as the idea of a national spirit or of a class spirit. The unity of the group was established on body-symbols that, though they are immanentist, are less clearly established on the reality of physical relationship, but build a body out of spiritual bonds.[13]

Finally, Voegelin pointed to another well-known development in European history, the particularization of the universal Christian community. The emergence of national kingships and national identities based on geographic, linguistic, and historical considerations,

12. *Ibid.*, 292; *RS,* 139.
13. Voegelin, "Growth of the Race Idea," 293; *RS,* 140.

and the parallel evolution of ideas of territorial royal sovereignty fragmented the idea of the universal church that spiritually united Europe. The church structure itself began to disintegrate in conjunction with the emerging secular particularization when national sovereigns succeeded in making the ecclesiastical realm coextensive with the political realm through the formation of national churches. The creation of the Church of England by Henry VIII is the best-known and clearest example of this development.

If we join together the trends of secularization with the immanentist transformation of the image of life, first in the biological and then in the anthropological fields, a new set of symbols begins to emerge. The spiritual bond of the community has become immanent as has the nature and unfolding of the individual. The process of immanentization means that the immanent, spiritual symbols are no longer Christian in any sense of the word, but "residuums," and "because of their essentially fragmentary character, they are capable of evolving almost any new set of symbols out of the elements that are offered by the civilizational situation of the moment." [14] In our case, the strength of body-ideas is combined with a biological discourse of race to produce emotionally persuasive symbols, and eventually, ideologies of race.

Linking a series of events or ideas together to form a meaningful account of their development is not equivalent to determining the final causes of the appearance of one and the gradual disappearance of another. Ideas do not replace one another in an absolute sense, but emerge out of one another as the content of one, informed by the archetypes and philosophical discourses of the day, is changed, and leads to a new symbol. [15] What the underlying causes of the change are is indeterminable, although the experiential motivation may be more accessible to analysis. [16] We are not interested in causes here, but in describing the transformation of one complex of meaning into another on the basis of a series of events that we can locate, even if we cannot explain them in accordance with the criteria of causal

14. Voegelin, "Growth of the Race Idea," 294.
15. *Ibid.*
16. *RI,* 14. "For one cannot decide whether new community-ideas and their growth were the causes for the suppression of the older ones, or if a tiring of the older ideas created the space in which new ones that would otherwise have been integrated, expanded, spreading out independently" (*RS,* 139).

logic. The strength of the ideas of process and immanent teleology (the latter an anthropomorphism injected into the idea of random evolution) that arise from the notion of species development, can be seen in Voegelin's discovery of analogies of organism and organic growth applied to the social structures of the community or the nation.[17]

RACE AND STATE

An account of historical events begins with one's own community, but it must also incorporate into its story the existence of other communities and their relationship to our own; our earlier example from the Exodus narrative is a case in point. We examined Voegelin's method of ordering historical events so that configurations of meaning could be derived from them, and found that reality could not be "ordered and mastered" in rational categories at all, but that threads of meaning imposed their own meaning, within their own historical context, on the observer. We also noted that the "expansion of the historical horizon," to use Voegelin's phrase, was a determining factor in transforming the archetype of human nature. For the men who were attempting to make sense of the manifold of new historical and geographical material, which was forever destroying the ethnocentricity of European historical self-understanding, some ordering principle had to be found. One possibility, though by no means the only one, was the symbol of race; it was already in use as a form of classification of human types earlier in the nineteenth century (*RS*, 156), and could perhaps now be used as a category for explaining the broad, segregated expanse of history. As in all iconic and archetypical transformations, the shift to an explanation of history on the basis of race from other, less deterministic constructions was a gradual one (*RS*, 157). But by the early nineteenth century, writers such as Gobineau were explaining the course of history in terms of the organic unfolding and interrelationships of various human races.

The problem of "making sense of existence" in a way that would be coherent and meaningful for politics was addressed by Voegelin in consideration of the rise of what he called particularistic communities. We have already considered closely the kinds of speculative

17. *RS*, 139. For example, see Arthur de Gobineau, *The Inequality of the Human Races*, trans. Adrian Collins (New York, 1967), 24, 26.

constructions that, under an immanent archetype of human life and human community, would make sense of the complex of relationships between the individual and the community. They, however, are only half of the equation. Now we must consider the relationship of distinct communities to one another under an immanentist archetype informed by race-ideas.

DEATH AND MEANING

The Exodus narrative, as said earlier, served to locate its community in space and time. The community achieves its clearest distinctiveness in the narrative when it is contrasted with other communities. Pharaoh's act of speaking, by which he divides the world into distinct political spheres, creates the tension in the framework on which the ensuing narrative is strung. This particularization of mankind into distinct groups is taken up by Jahweh, who then acts on that basis, representing and aiding one group against another and its gods and rulers. An immanentist theory of race does not permit a god to act on behalf of any particular community nor, for that matter, on behalf of mankind in general. The processes and forces that determine a community and its characteristics are immanent to it and to mankind. Voegelin found in the writings of Schelling a consideration of the problem of "fear" or "anxiety" that results from men's experience of the disruption of unity when "mankind" is sundered into discrete groups that stand in opposition to one another.[18] Voegelin carefully described the meaning of the term as he found it in Schelling:

> We must not misunderstand *Angst* as a precaution to preserve unity, but rather, we must understand it in its existential meaning bestowed on it by Schelling as an agitation in which the whole of existence is experienced as fatally threatened not through an attack from a particular external direction, but from within through a metaphysical annihilation of existence, as a horror not only of earthly death, but of total destruction. Schelling thereby describes the psychic state into which men fall when they, either in passing or constantly, lose their connection to the world in one or another or all the strata of their being. (*RS*, 152)

18. Friedrich W. J. Schelling, *Einleitung in die Philosophie der Mythologie* (Munich, 1928). The German word for "anxiety" here is *Angst*. We should resist ascribing to this German term the conceptual baggage that has accrued to it from its usage in psychological theories and Heideggerian speculation.

126

Such a loss of connection to the world may occur when men become aware of their commonality with other men (symbolized by "mankind"), yet at the same time experience division into "partial unities" within which they may seek to restore an even greater sense of unity of the part in order to overcome their feeling of loss at the disintegration of the whole (*RS*, 151).

We cannot enter into a full consideration here of the correctness of what Voegelin assumed to be Schelling's accurate analysis of a basic human experience and responses to it. Research conducted in the relatively new discipline of thanatology, however, does indicate that Voegelin had uncovered an important theme. Robert Lifton and Eric Olson, for example, have indicated, in an interesting study on the human experience of death and attempts to symbolize its meaning, that "without a cultural context in which life has continuity and boundaries . . . but when individual life appears to lack significance beyond itself, death becomes profoundly threatening, unacceptable." [19] Death becomes acceptable when an "emotional context or system of meaning" is available that will make death mean more than individual extinction. "To live in the face of inevitable death, man requires a sense that his life has continuity and significance." Consequently, an individual's existence remains meaningful and retains a sense of vitality "only so long as the symbolizing process provides forms and images adequate to guide behavior and render it meaningful." [20] We claimed earlier that providing forms and images, insofar as it integrated the individual life into a story of the whole, was a central purpose of narrative.

As the Christian archetype of the whole, with its symbols and its vision of the reality of the transcendent, faded away,[21] what Lifton calls the "struggle to achieve a sense of continuity and significance" arising out of the "human need for a sense of historical connection beyond the individual's life" became more visible and intense.[22]

19. Robert J. Lifton and Eric Olson, *Living and Dying* (New York, 1974), 28.
20. *Ibid.*, 25, 31.
21. Voegelin noted that despite such unifying Christian symbols, the Christian archetype and the [general] history of the Christian religion were also characterized by a diminished view of the "cosmic-vital connection between man and nature that begets a constant readiness, in comparison with other cultures and times, to give room to experiences of isolation, of lostness, and of desolation" (*RS*, 152).
22. Lifton and Olson, *Living and Dying*, 61, 75. For a condensed account of shifts in archetypes as they relate to the view of the relationship between death and

Lifton and Olson found this need for historical connection to be expressed in five different types of what they called "modes of symbolic immortality." They defined symbolic immortality as the "psychological process of creating meaningful images . . . adequate to give a sense of significance to experience." Part of the product of symbolic immortality, then, is equivalent to Voegelin's theoretical category of political ideas. Symbols of immortality give significance to experience by "reflecting man's relatedness to all that comes before him and all that follows him." "Without this unending sense of attachment to aim and principles beyond the self . . . the capacity to feel at home in the world . . . cannot be sustained." [23] Here again we may be reminded of a parallel purpose in political ideas of the community. A loss of this sense of attachment, as described by Lifton and Olson, leads to the *Angst* Voegelin discovered in Schelling's work, if "attachment" includes a purposeful sense of the whole, of mankind in its unity with the cosmos, or universe, or world.

The five modes of symbolic mortality that Lifton and Olson cataloged were: biological immortality; human "works," or creative immortality; theological immortality; continuity with nature; and experiential transcendence. The primary mode of interest to us here is the first: biological immortality. Lifton and Olson called it the "most obvious" mode, and it is one with which we are by now thoroughly familiar. Its major components include symbols of generational continuity, reproductive continuity, the family "name," and other body-symbols that symbolically integrate the individual into the community and that symbolically create a political-communal unity.

There is a kind of *Angst* that results from the experienced dissolution of mankind into discrete groups that each searches for its meaning in the context of the whole of mankind. The more narrow importance of this kind of *Angst* for race-ideas and race theory is that "the particular community overcomes its fear (*Angst*) of its own lostness by positing itself as 'world' and everything else as 'non-world' in contrast to itself." Consequently, *Angst* may be "the deepest root of the new community-idea in its individual characteristics" (*RS*, 153).

---

community, see Kenneth A. Harris, "The Political Meaning of Death: An Existential Overview," *Omega*, II (1971), 227–39.

23. Lifton and Olson, *Living and Dying*, 76.

Out of fear, according to Voegelin, arise "the hatred against the opposing worlds that can, by their sheer existence throw me back at any moment into the experience of fear" (*RS*, 153). Out of this fear arise also the "radical divisions" between the "kingdoms of good and evil" that translate into various symbols in race theories of good and evil races.

Interestingly, Lifton and Olson also described a subcategory of "biological immortality" that they called "biosocial immortality." Observing correctly that "because man is the 'cultural animal,' the biological mode can never remain purely biological," Lifton recognized also "the fine line between love of country and people on the one hand, and hatefilled, violent nationalism on the other." [24] Voegelin attributed the hatred and its consequent radical particularization to fear engendered by an inability to cope moderately with the sense of dissolution that the breakup of the species "mankind" into smaller groups might bring about. It was not the case that *all* theories of race embodied such violence and hatred, just as it is not the case that love of country and one's own people necessarily leads to virulent nationalism. Many race theories were of this nature, however, and Voegelin presumed to have found at least a partial explanation for their character in the motivations that led to symbolizations of continuity and immortality of both individuals and, more especially, of communities. Although corroboration is not equivalent to confirmation, the studies of Lifton and Olson as well as other thanatologists indicate that Voegelin's estimation of the importance of Schelling's *Angst* for the formation of community-ideas was not without foundation.

RACE-IDEAS AND NARRATIVE: SYMBOL AND FUNCTION

The transformation of the mystical "body of Christ" into the nation also led to the organizational articulation of the nation in the form of the state and its various apparatuses. Accordingly, Voegelin transferred the title of *Rasse und Staat* internally to the second half of this work, where he dealt specifically with the political forms that race-ideas assumed in the context of the European state system. We need not replicate here the minutiae of Voegelin's summary analysis of the various political theories of race that he examined. It is important, however, to note what he found to be the common principal

24. Robert J. Lifton, *The Broken Connection* (New York, 1979), 19, 20.

129

themes and ideas in all of them. Comparing these with the principal themes and purposes of narrative discussed earlier, and keeping in mind the possible role of *Angst* in the formation of new community symbols, we will see how such theories of race lead to archetypical transformations in the way men think about themselves *politically* and about the political world they inhabit. Understanding such a transformation, moreover, leads to at least a partial understanding of the emergence of ideologies that led to death camps.

In the last paragraph of the fourth chapter of the second part of *Rasse und Staat,* Voegelin concluded that the transformation of Christian community-ideas into the idea of the particularistic community and the motivating role of *Angst* in the development of ideas concerning those outside one's own particularist community together constituted the basic schema into which all the segmented parts of the entire *anthropos* of the new immanent archetype could be inserted. All that remained was to "study the details" of how this schema could be "filled in by body-ideas" (*RS,* 154).

Voegelin then proceeded to outline a simple schematic that characterized the "major type of the political race-idea." The decisive division is between the weak and the strong (or the active and the passive) races; the implications of this division constitute the mechanism by which history "unfolds." Races migrate, which leads to racial encounters, and to the subjugation of the weaker (or more passive) by the stronger (or more active). A result of this conquest is that the two kinds of races in any given historical instance will develop a symbiotic relationship that in turn is the foundation of all great societies in history. The symbiosis is typically thought to end either through assimilation or the numerical suppression of the stronger by the weaker, so that a situation of equality between the two eventually develops. The "worth to civilization" of this last development constitutes the major point of dissension in race theory (*RS,* 167–68). Cast in such a schematic, and set in the context of a particularist community trying to make sense of its place in a world of many other such apparently segmented communities, this "major type of the political race-idea" can be shown to fulfill similar functions (in any of its variations) to those of the Exodus narrative.

In the previous chapter we saw that as the immanent archetype of man and human community emerged through the full development of an immanent archetype of the natural world, it introduced both problems and solutions with regard to the meaning and purposes of

130

individual and collective human existence. We have now seen that to be effectively accepted, this same immanent archetype had also to encompass and order, for those who accept it, the relationships between two or more distinct communities. Accordingly, the political ideas of man and community expressed in the terms of this archetype served the same purposes as ideas of man and community expressed in the terms of the symbols and actions of the Jewish Exodus and the Christian Gospel narratives. These same purposes, however, were not served in the same way.

The differences between narrative and theory may be indicated by describing them as activities. To narrate is to tell a story. Its purpose, to repeat, is "that some story is needed to give a person's life-experience coherence and continuity over time—else there can be only the experience of nothingness."[25] A story sets the context for determining who we are, what we are about, and for telling us the way the world is. To be sure, we can analyze the various "components" that together constitute a story, such as the plot, characters, style, narrator's perspective, and so on. This, however, is not to *tell* a story, but to analyze it.

To theorize is to consider a topic, event, or phenomenon in terms of analytical categories that presumably serve to uncover the fundamental structures and meanings of the object under consideration. To theorize is to eliminate from consideration, at least initially, the incidental aspect of what is being considered and to focus on those characteristics of it that the theorist regards as essential and that allow the theorist to compare and contrast it with other objects. Presence and absence, more than and less than, alike and unalike, for example, are three pairs of basic categories that allow us to theorize about phenomena and compare them with other phenomena. To theorize, then, is not to tell a story about something or someone, but to analyze it, to categorize it, and to comprehend its meaning, structure, and "essence" by such means. Just as there can be good and bad storytelling, there can be good and bad theorizing. To disregard important elements of a phenomenon or to disregard important questions of meaning regarding a phenomenon are two methods of bad theorizing that Voegelin uncovered in his examination of race theories.

In the preceding chapter we encountered briefly a number of the

25. Hauerwas, *Peaceable Kingdom*, 32.

functions that political race-ideas serve, parallel to those of the Exodus narrative. There we saw that the body-ideas of ascent, descent,
generation, and biological relation, all of which stand out particularly in our passage from the Exodus narrative, are also the central
themes around which are grouped the main explanatory and symbolic
problems of immanentist race- and body-ideas. Body-ideas, we have
said, are frequently an important set of political ideas that provide a
context for self-understanding, and a means of symbolic unity to a
given community. We recall that the importance of race-ideas in this
respect is that they incorporate immanentized body-ideas, in which
the body, both actual biological and political-mythical, and its functions and purposes are explained in terms of the immanent species.

Confining ourselves to specific functions, we noted that narrative
provides individuals with an understanding of human existence and
its meaning, an understanding that is directed toward the "aggregate
experience of a whole human community." [26] We have already seen
the tension between the purposes of the individual and the purposes
of the community with which race theory wrestled in trying to explain systematically the political content of race-ideas. According to
Voegelin, the "schema of race theory" is manifested when "the belief in divine activity" is taken away from the idea of the "naturally
determined inequality of people" and replaced with a notion of the
natural (immanent) characteristic of the body (RS, 145). Moreover,
in the former Christian notions of the Kingdom of God, all were
servants of a higher cause or ideal, each in his or her own capacity.
When this notion of the Kingdom of God becomes immanentized
into the idea of the nation or nation-state and is used for political
purposes, "the relationship between the kingdom (of God) and serv-
ice in its behalf is . . . transformed into its opposite; the world exists for the sake of the few God-sent individuals, and the rest are
to be their instruments. Moreover, the overwhelming majority of
people do not even belong to the kingdom as servants, but stand outside it, opposed to it as the enemy that spurs the well-intentioned
on to new efforts. The greatest part of mankind has its place in
the world plan only as the foils for an elite of godded men" (RS,
145–46). We then have the possibilities for new speculative understandings concerning the individual's relationship to the community
as elaborated previously.

26. Goldberg, *Jews and Christians*, 26.

The second element of the narrative, we said, was its self-identification with a human particularity. Here, too, we already have indicated some of the effects of immanentization on the community's understanding of itself. It is no longer dependent on the divine for its existence, nor does it serve as an agent or representative on earth of a divine being.[27] Such a community may, nevertheless, remain the bearing vessel for secular truths such as liberalism, communism, socialism, or other systematic, ideological conceptions of the truth of human existence.[28] Societies for whom the truth of their existence is articulated in terms of ideas of the immanent species will understand themselves in terms of conceptions of immanent intraspecies development and conflict. The important point here, however, is that race theorists do not tell *stories* about particular events or personalities or conflicts between peoples or races, but spin out speculative themes and broad, generalized explanations of how one race comes to dominate another. Let us remember that the concept of race in all such speculations remains unclear to a lesser or greater extent, as do frequently the historical details. In the narrative that we examined, the opposite is the case. Narrative is the recounting of a particular event, or of the acts of a particular person or group, or of these in combination. Narrative is not speculative, schema-building, or broadly explanatory. Narrative does not deal directly with broad forces in history and speculative constructions about how these forces, embodied in groups of people or select individuals, interact. Although archetypes incorporating such broader, species views of human existence may *underlie* a narrative, a narrative embedded in such an archetype would nevertheless remain a story about one or a series of contingent events and the individuals who initiate and suffer them; it would *not* be a speculative construction of the type we call race theory or of any other type. It would be a story.

When race theorists do speculate at the level of the individual, it is in terms of "types," such as the "Nordic type," the "Normanic type," the "Oriental type," and so on. At the level of the community, its character and purpose are, once again, expressed discursively in terms of the *idea* directly, not through the medium of a

27. For an enlightening example of such representation, see Eric Voegelin, "The Mongol Orders of Submission to European Powers, 1245–1255," *Byzantion*, XI (1941), 378–413.

28. Voegelin's discussion of such representation may be found in *New Science*, *passim*.

story or a series of stories. Voegelin concentrated particularly on the "Nordic idea," which, expressed historically, is the idea "that there is one race, the Nordic, that excels above all others, and is responsible for the cultural achievements of Occidental and a great portion of Oriental mankind." Expressed politically, it is the idea "that the Nordic racial elements of the population are to be promoted by sociopolitical means" (RS, 215). The Nordic idea was cast in varying, sometimes contradictory political-cultural forms.[29] Voegelin reported that the idea could be traced in its roots all the way back to Linnaeus; from his time forward, numerous classifications of race and at least as numerous interpretations of their meaning could be found.

The "Nordic idea" was only one of many speculative constructions of race appearing in the nineteenth century that had political influence. Considering them all together, Voegelin noted that "the complex itself of the race-ideas is a chaotic web of every type of construction that can be derived from the material data" (RS, 214–15). All used race-ideas and body-ideas to explain the purposes, structures, and meanings of particular communities and of the role of the individual in his/her particular community. All presumed to have the character of science insofar as they took the form of scientific theories (even if their authors strove to give them much more authority than scientists pretended for their theories and hypotheses) and incorporated with greater or lesser precision conceptual elements of various natural and social sciences (RS, 209). Voegelin concluded of them that their "theoretical niveau" was "rather modest" (RS, 210), itself a charitable but otherwise hardly surprising summation, given his earlier investigation of their foundations.

We observed a third comparison between narrative and race theory: that the Exodus narrative located its subjects in space and time, and thereby helped also to locate both those who told it and those who heard and accepted it as their own in a particular (meaningful) location at a specific time. A parallel function for race theories is somewhat more difficult to discern, since races and especially "types" are less geographically and historically distinct than particularist communities articulated to action in leadership structures and possessing a distinct cultural and historical tradition. We recall

29. See RS, 218–25.

that the mixing of races is a key theme in what Voegelin found to be the basic paradigm of race theory. Indeed, more than one race theory he investigated was concerned with the various racial strata its author presumed to find in a single community.[30]

Events and actions take place in discrete spaces and at discrete times. Because they do not concern themselves with events or actions of individuals, but tend to concern themselves with the broad forces of race conflict and mutual influence, usually clothing their speculations in the language derived from various sciences, race theorists tend to locate the individual within those forces, not in discrete locations in space and time. Except for the few gifted, great men, who are an expression of the excellence of the race, the individual members of a race are regarded more as constituents of a mass in motion that embodies the characteristics of the race than as individuals who live out a tradition of which, living in a community that bears this tradition, they are an integral part. In this restricted sense, then, when confronted with an individual human being, race theory is a-historical.[31]

A fourth element of narrative, we said, was that it distinguished one community and its traditions, gods, and heroes from another. The parallel in race theory has been sufficiently considered in our discussion of the particularist immanent community and its symbols. We may note here that Voegelin offered an extended discussion in *Rasse und Staat* of one particular idea of this variety, namely "the Jews as counteridea" (*RS*, 186–208). Once again, the concern is not with individuals and their deeds, but with types, who do not do deeds or act, but simply *are* a certain way, expressing in their behavior racially predetermined characteristics.

We have completed the discussion of Eric Voegelin's investigation of race as a political symbol in modernity. What remains now is to indicate the role of this immanentist symbol in modern totalitarian regimes.

30. See *RS*, 212–14.
31. We should note here that all dialectical theology in the Christian tradition notwithstanding, the essence of that religion is rooted in a historical tradition, namely the incarnation, death, and resurrection of Jesus Christ. All Christian speculation, even that which denies all three of these elements to be historical in a concrete sense, begins in this tradition, even if only in the form of a rejection of it.

SIX

The Logic of the Race-Idea

Contingent, historical events cannot be separated from the ideas that inform the society constituted by those events. Consequently, when we speak of the ideas that inform totalitarianism, we must remember that these ideas appeal to a certain kind of psyche. Minds are shaped not only by sheer, unconnected ideas, but by particular kinds of continuous, persistent experiences. This is not to say that all events and responses to them are determined, but that it is likely that we will encounter certain spiritual and intellectual formations in history that we may be able to trace back to certain specific events that in turn arose out of other formations, developed through earlier events, and so on in an orderly configuration. Events and the essence of a society are intimately linked. Voegelin concentrated chiefly on essence, as this essay has reflected. To maintain an evenhanded perspective, however, we must recognize that totalitarianism is not only a configuration of essences or ideas, but also a concrete event that brings the ideas that inform it to actuality. It is further dependent for its appearance on other contingent events as well as on ideas that shape the social landscape in such a way as to enable its emergence into the world. Examining the ideas that inform an event will give us a deeper understanding of it, but we must remember that ideas do not exist in a realm of their own; they are a part of a community that is also shaped by the actions of men.

Discerning important from unimportant events, so as to be able to give a coherent and meaningful account of what has happened, is partially a matter of skill and luck, and partially a matter of perspective. When Voegelin's books on race were published in 1933,

136

the term "totalitarian" was not applied with conceptual precision to any political regime: totalitarian regimes themselves had just appeared, and analysis of the new phenomenon was in its initial stages. Voegelin examined the metaphysical and systematic content of race ideas to determine their deficiencies as the spiritual and intellectual basis of a community, and it appears that he may have intuited their destructive capabilities (*RI*, 23), but he did not yet have knowledge of the full breadth of totalitarian regimes as events— for the obvious reason that the destructive capacities were indeed only capacities, not actualities. Hannah Arendt was able to analyze the totalitarian regimes after their appearance (and, in the example of Nazi Germany, its destruction); she could thus more closely scrutinize not only the ideas informing them, but also the accompanying social and political events that were brought to a head in the Nazi and Soviet regimes of the thirties and forties. In this final chapter, I will use Arendt's analysis where needed to fill in the gaps necessarily left in Voegelin's work. These gaps are not so great as one might imagine. Through his examination, we may readily isolate several strands of logic in race-ideas that give them the constituent form needed for totalitarian strategies.

TOTALITARIANISM

Arendt's work *The Origins of Totalitarianism* was an attempt to isolate, in her own words, the "elements which eventually crystallize into totalitarianism."[1] In locating these elements, some reaching back to the seventeenth century, Arendt also provided a partial study of the essence of totalitarianism. There are, of course, accounts of the genesis of totalitarianism other than Arendt's, just as other readings than mine of her *Origins of Totalitarianism* are possible.[2] Our focus, however, is on Voegelin, and we consider Arendt's work in the context of that focus.

The central idea shaping totalitarian regimes is motion. Almost all other facets of fully developed totalitarian regimes can be accounted for in terms of motion. The need for masses and media

1. Hannah Arendt, "A Reply" to Eric Voegelin's review of *The Origins of Totalitarianism*, by Hannah Arendt, in *Review of Politics*, XV (1953), 81.
2. See, for example, Robert Burrowes, "Totalitarianism: The Revised Standard Version," *World Politics*, XXI (1968), 272–80.

technology, concentration camps, amorphous governmental structure, a secret police, and terror, can all be attributed to the totalitarian program of transforming the stability of the state, social
classes, and even private relationships into a continual, massive
movement. Motion is the essence of totalitarian rule, and all other
phenomena related to the regime, including power, are focused on
and in movement.[3] To implement such motion, we require both the
right configuration of social factors (a mass society, leaders willing
to introduce the novel system, the necessary technologies of mental
and physical domination, and so on) as well as the political ideas
suitable for superseding political and historical existence with movement.[4] One implication of this argument is that not all political ideas
(even immanentist ones) are equally useful for implementing totalitarian motion. Indeed, some may be inimical to such intentions.

The idea of motion itself, according to Arendt, was introduced
into politics by the bourgeoisie in the eighteenth and nineteenth centuries. Originally an apolitical class of businessmen, the bourgeoisie
was interested only in endlessly increasing its wealth by expanding
its business opportunities. When it became clear that the established
structures of the state hampered their expansionist interests, its
members sought political power in an effort to protect and enhance
those interests. Their success in persuading their respective European home governments to protect their expansionism for the sake
of the wealth it would ostensibly create, meant that European states
became the custodians and representatives of an expansionist movement that was in fact the antithesis of the stability and order states
were initially intended to ensure and protect. According to Arendt,
the bourgeoisie were interested neither in politics per se, nor in stability, but in an ever-expanding cycle of expansion and consumption
for its own sake. The mood is summed up in Arendt's quote from
Cecil Rhodes, perhaps the greatest expansionist of them all: "I

3. Voegelin used the theoretical symbol of "seelische Aktivierung" in *Autoritäre Staat* (52) to account for the same central characteristic. For an early account
of the political tools used to generate and maintain mass homogeneity and motion,
see Sigmund Neumann, *Permanent Revolution: The Total State in a World at War*
(London, 1942), 118–229.
4. See Arendt, *Totalitarianism,* 460–68, and Carl J. Friedrich and Zbigniew
Brzezinski, *Totalitarian Dictatorship and Autocracy* (Cambridge, Mass., 1965),
16–17.

would annex the planets if I could."[5] Arendt argued that the introduction of expansion for its own sake as a policy of government developed into several of the social institutions and intellectual forces that coalesced in totalitarian regimes. The most important of these for our analysis were the ideas of a "never-ending accumulation of property," and the "never-ending accumulation of power" necessary for the protection of the former. Together, they were the two basic ideas underlying imperialism, which in turn could easily be transformed into the more abstract ideas of motion and eternal process.[6]

IDEOLOGY

The term *ideology* has been understood in any number of ways. For our purposes, it is, very simply, a scientific speech (*logos*) about an idea.[7] Those who engage in ideological discussion believe it is possible to treat ideas like the objects of a phenomenal science, implying that we can make scientific statements about them. On the basis of our earlier analysis, we can say that ideology therefore begins with a category error.

One of the principles of natural science is that an acceptable scientific hypothesis must be able to produce reliable predictions about the outcome of a particular set of physical conditions. An experiment may be defined as the manufacture of a set of phenomenal conditions to test a hypothesis concerning the causal relationship of those conditions and the effects they produce on each other. For example, when Albert Einstein published his theory of relativity, other physicists tested it not only for its internal mathematical coherence and plausiblity, but the Royal Society and the Royal Astronomical Society in London, England, devised an experiment to test the theory empirically as well. Einstein's theory predicted that light would be bent when it passed near a strong gravitational field. An eclipse of the sun in 1919 was used to take measurements of how much the rays of light from a star passing through the sun's gravitational field

5. S. Gertrude Millin, *Rhodes* (London, 1933), 138, quoted in Arendt, *Totalitarianism*, 124.
6. For a summary account of the process of bourgeoisie political emancipation and the institutions and ideas that sprang from it, see Barry Cooper, *The End of History: An Essay on Modern Hegelianism* (Toronto, 1984), 14–19.
7. The following discussion is derived from Arendt, *Totalitarianism*, 468–70.

are bent. The experiment confirmed Einstein's predictions. This understanding of scientific method has been taught as basic training to generations of high-school pupils.[8]

Ideologists invert the scientific principle of predictability in two ways. First, they treat an idea like a concept, and then, reducing the idea to a single premise, they proceed to make deductions from it. The idea is lifted from history, and history is then made the subject matter of the ideology. The deductions made from the ideological premise become comprehensive revelations about the order of history. On the basis of these logical deductions from a premise derived from an idea, ideologists claim to be able to explain everything in history. An ideology treats the historical succession of events "as if it followed the same 'law' as the logical exposition of its idea."[9] The "laws" of ideology are the laws of an unfolding, ongoing process. An ideology does not claim to be truth-speaking primarily on the basis of observation, experience, or reflection, but on the basis of the presentation of the logical system itself. It is a complete discourse that does not require empirical verification or thinking to substantiate its claims, but only the logical unfolding of deductions from its single premise. The logic of the system becomes its own verification.

Second, natural scientists, in principle, remain passive in their predictions of events. In other words, if a hypothesis predicts a particular phenomenon under a given set of conditions, and the phenomenon does not appear, then the hypothesis is modified or discarded. Ideologists invert this methodological principle by manufacturing the results of their deductions if they are not otherwise forthcoming. Therefore, though their proponents claim to use a "scientific approach" in their deductive explanation of history, ideologies are para-political; they arise in a world of ordinary, commonsense politics, and therefore contain a component of intent (namely, to replace the world of politics where they first appear). By the use of the Greek prefix *para* I mean to imply that ideologists are not, strictly speaking, political people, in the sense of being open to rational discussion, engaged in a search for an order, and

8. The story is related in R. W. Reid, *Tongues of Conscience: War and the Scientists' Dilemma* (London, 1970), 47–48.
9. Arendt, *Totalitarianism*, 469.

willing to make compromises on the basis of conflicting interests. Ideologists are more akin to technicians with a blueprint that gives them the instructions, as it were, for making a new world with new men in it. Political intent is transformed through the scientistic superstitions inherent in ideologies into a program of making logical deductions come true. For example: let it be given that Germans are the "Aryan master race." It follows that German scientific achievement is greater than that of any other race. The proof is that there are no first-rate non-German scientists and scientific theories. The proof is tested and shown to be valid when all non-German scientists are liquidated and their theories disregarded.[10] The logical consequences of ideologies become the policy proposals of their proponents. Ideology is the intellectual component of the totalitarian programme.

RACE AND MYSTERY

As we have seen, Voegelin traced the genealogy of the race-idea from its beginnings in a transcendental conception of life to the modern, atheistic, immanentist archetype of the biosphere. Not only the race-idea itself, but also the body-ideas of which it is one, underwent a similar transformation. Voegelin, we recall, argued that political ideas of community based on experiences of the body are a constituent part of the complex of symbols of any community. He illustrated their transformation by tracing body-ideas from the classical Greek gentilitian body-ideas of *anchisteia, genos, phratria,* and *demos* to the idea of the mystical body of Christ and from there into the modern idea of the nation.[11]

When the spiritual bonds, the purpose, and the development of the community become entirely immanent, both in terms of the lives of its members, and of the community as a whole, it becomes more tempting and easier to reject the aspects of mystery residing in the ontological nature of human beings, and to consider the completely immanent to be completely knowable. God no longer holds in His hand the secret of life; the "secret of life" is no longer a secret, but an immanent phenomenon with its own immanent laws

10. See Reid, *Tongues of Conscience,* 58–59, for an example of such policy in action.

11. The account may be found in *RS,* 127–54. Voegelin's "Growth of the Race Idea" provides an excellent English summary (286–94).

of existence and continuation. Consequently, we may come to believe that we can penetrate its mystery, that in fact, it is a mystery in appearance only. We have already seen the ontological impossibility of such thinking, but a loss of experiences of transcendence makes the attempt more likely to be persuasive, at least in part. The reasons behind the drive to penetrate the mystery of being are manifold; we will consider one of them presently. Voegelin believed that both the advance in knowledge and the technological successes of the natural sciences greatly assisted the attempt to reduce everything to an object of the phenomenal sciences; technological success, a kind of "proof of the pudding," as it were, paved the way for claims that complete explanations of things could be and would be forthcoming.[12]

The reductionist attempts themselves point to a theme that lies near the surface of Voegelin's discussion. In the course of the present essay, we have encountered a long series of examples of a refusal to ask or answer certain questions. The use of "vague expressions" to deflect vital ontological questions (*RS*, 78), a disregard for methodological problems (*RS*, 74, 84), a scientistic insistence that metaphysical questions of method and ontology may be disregarded (*RS*, 35, 92), and a general imprecision in the application of concepts and methods (*RS*, 91), are all signs of a deterioration, brought on by scientistic dogma, in theoretical considerations. In some instances, these indicators are quite clearly conscious rejections of theoretical problems (*RS*, 74, 81, 84). A rejection of this kind, however, is properly to be understood as evidence that the mystery remains firmly in place; though certain kinds of explanations and constructions of things may give the illusion of penetrating through the mystery or of opening it up, the speciousness of the claim is evident from its basis in a denial of theoretical questions. The denial is in turn made evident by analysis of the kind undertaken by Voegelin.

RACE AND HISTORY

Voegelin once commented that he did not have a philosophy of history. Something resembling a philosophy of history, however, can be gleaned from the introductions to the first, second, and fourth volumes of his *Order and History*.[13] Furthermore, Voegelin appar-

12. Voegelin, *Autoritäre Staat*, 105–106.
13. Sebba, "Prelude and Variations," 4.

ently considered Thomas Mann's *Joseph und seine Brüder* to "offer one of the great philosophies of history of our time." The opening lines of that work read, "Deep is the well of the past. Should we not call it unfathomable?" [14] The waters of the bottomless well are constituted by various elements, of which Voegelin identified several. The point was that history is neither a graspable object, nor simply a topic of study. To "do" history is to tell stories about great men and great deeds. To study history is to review the stories, their meaning, and their revelations of the order of human existence.

In his later years, Voegelin called history the "process in which man articulates his own nature"; [15] his major work, the five-volume *Order and History,* is largely an examination of that articulation. This notion of history was already present in *Die Rassenidee in der Geistesgeschichte;* there the substance of history was the actions of the archetypical man (*RI,* 21). We noted earlier that an archetype must be embodied in an individual before it can be visible to the many. The stories of such men and their actions are the substance of history; they establish or sustain the ideas and the structures of a political community. Human experience becomes "history" when it is articulated in narrative. Consciousness (the primal manner of seeing) determines being (the manner of existence and of understanding existence). Speech and action are revelations of human consciousness and the subject matter of the stories that are the fabric of history. Thus, history is not directed toward an end, but is a symbol for the recurring quest for an order of being found in human consciousness. History as a topic is nothing more than the story of the quest, revealed in the speech and actions of great men who, by words and deeds, disclosed their souls to others. [16]

If historical experience becomes articulated ideologically, however, the conception of the nature of history itself is changed. History may become the logical expression of a particular idea (ideology) such as race conflict or class conflict. As the expression of the logic of an idea, history becomes fully graspable; its essence, meaning, and direction can be discovered and articulated with the same kind of certainty that it could if it were an object of scientific

14. Webb, *Eric Voegelin,* 17; Thomas Mann, *Joseph und seine Brüder* (Frankfurt am Main, 1960), 9, Vol. VI of Mann, *Gesammelte Werke.*
15. *OH* I, 2.
16. See also Hannah Arendt, *The Human Condition* (Chicago, 1958), 181–92.

study. If the forces that propel human history can be discovered and articulated, then, based on the logic of the idea that embodies them, history—that is, the doings of men—can be manipulated to make it "come out right." We no longer tell stories, but manipulate what were formerly their subjects, contents, and meaning. A literary example may serve us here.

In *Darkness at Noon,* Arthur Koestler describes the psychological journey of a man who has come to doubt the logic of an idea to which he has devoted his entire life. Indeed, the very possibility of any such logic of any idea is in doubt. Rubashov, the doubter, has been arrested on the suspicion of his doubt; such doubt is dangerous to those who wish to implement the logic of an idea sociopolitically, *i.e.,* in the manner we have described. Koestler describes the relationship between history and knowers largely through Rubashov in several scenes both before and during his imprisonment, and also through Ivanov, one of his interrogators.[17]

Rubashov gives us the first major introduction to the theme. "The Party," he declares, "is the embodiment of the revolutionary idea in history. History knows no scruples and no hesitation. Inert and unerring, she flows towards her goal. At every bend in her course she leaves the mud which she carries and the corpses of the drowned. History knows her way. She makes no mistakes. He who has not absolute faith in History does not belong in the Party's ranks."[18] The anthropomorphism should remind us of similar tendencies we observed when some race theorists and evolutionists describe the forces of evolution. The Party, namely, those who understand the workings of history and those who carry out the policies arising out of such understanding, knows its topic—history—and has grasped its (her) logic. Indeed, the Party's policy and deeds "embody" this logic; expressed another way, they embody "the will of history," which is "the revolutionary idea."[19]

17. Arthur Koestler, *Darkness at Noon* (New York, 1941). The focal ideology in Koestler's story is "classism," "the ideology which interprets history as an economic struggle of classes." I consider racism, the ideology "that interprets history as a natural fight of races," to be sufficiently similar in its logical structure and policy outcomes that transposition from one to the other is possible without noticeable distortion (see Arendt, *Totalitarianism,* 159).

18. Koestler, *Darkness,* 34. See also 64.

19. *Ibid.,* 46.

The specific policy proposals generated by those who understand is described by Rubashov as "doing the work of prophets without their gift;" the Party "replaces vision by logical deduction."[20] History may be understood as embodying a set of axioms of motion: get the axioms right, and you will have correct public policy, that is, public policy that accords with the natural forces and direction of history.

The second element of interest in this manipulation of the logic of history is the experiment. If it is true that we understand the logic of the driving forces of the historical idea, it may also be the case that we do not understand it *absolutely*. To test empirically that which we claim to know theoretically is the purpose of scientific experimentation. Ivanov, Rubashov's interrogator, points out that "several million people [die] senselessly and pointlessly" every year through the catastrophes that nature visits on mankind in the form of drought, floods, earthquakes, and other natural disasters. Why, then, should those who have knowledge of history's inner workings "shrink from sacrificing a few hundred thousand for the most promising experiment in history"? To "liquidate the parasitic part of the peasantry" (one may assume the "parasitic part" to mean those peasants who live on the "wrong side" of historical necessity) by letting it die of starvation is a "necessary surgical operation." The operation is not at all senseless or pointless—it is to put into practice our theoretical knowledge, to test and verify it, and that is surely worth a few hundred thousand lives.[21] The experiments of ideological public policy give direction and focus to what is considered to be a previously directionless and meaningless existence. For racists, therefore, public policy may require some or many to die in the interests of racial eugenics, racial purity, or racial improvement and advancement.

If the logic of an idea imposes on us an axiomatic set of policy prescriptions, then death becomes the only argument available to us when the persuasiveness of the historically absolute idea fails.[22] Those who oppose the chosen race, master race, or whatever race is the focal point of historical unfolding, do so not on voluntary

20. *Ibid.*, 80–81.
21. See *Ibid.*, 131–32.
22. *Ibid.*, 129.

grounds, but because they are not of the "right" race. Their opposition is predetermined racially, or, put another way, genetically. Accordingly, the only possible responses to such an involuntary resistance against a race's appointed role in history are radical segregation, enslavement, or extermination. The logic of the absolute idea of racial conflict in history does not permit tolerance and cohabitation, unless the theory of such an idea posits cohabitation to result in "better" racial qualities than if one race dominated. In the latter case, if the idea is absolutized, tolerance and cohabitation would then become ideals to be realized above all else and at any cost.[23] In the one regime that embraced the logic of race conflict totally, however, ideologically prescribed death became the norm.

The political mendacity of the logic of an idea may be made clearer yet. The terror of a totalitarian regime in a community begins "when real enemies have been exterminated, and the search for 'objective enemies' starts up." An "objective enemy" is one whose status as enemy is "defined by the policy of the government," and not by his intent to commit a crime or to overthrow the regime. Accordingly, the police forces of totalitarian regimes do not arrest criminal suspects or investigate crimes, but arrest "categories of people" whose "criminal status" is not determined by anything they have done or intended to do, but by government policy (originating in the logic of a particular idea) dictating that to be who they are is to be an enemy of the regime.[24] In the case of race, who one is is determined by one's parentage. Culpability, therefore, does not depend on one's deeds, but is entirely a matter of historical fate. It is the role of racist policy merely to direct the forces of the regime to deal with such culpability in accordance with the dictates of the logic of the particular race-idea it embodies.

Because the race-idea in its immanent form is an idea that includes the notion of biological process and struggle for survival (introduced through the immanent archetypes of the biosphere we have already discussed), to take up this idea with absolute seriousness

23. "From the viewpoint of an organization which functions according to the principle that whoever is not included is excluded, whoever is not with me is against me, the world at large loses all the nuances, differentiations, and pluralistic aspects which had in any event become confusing and unbearable to the masses who had lost their place and their orientation in it" (Arendt, *Totalitarianism*, 381).

24. *Ibid.*, 422–24.

and without the intervening moderation of other nonprocess political ideas is to attempt to manifest sociopolitically the idea of biological process and struggle in the everyday world of human community. Society is set in motion, imitating the processes of species development and struggle for biological supremacy as articulated in the theories of Darwin and others under the immanentist archetype. Since the biological struggle for survival and further species development is seen in these natural-scientific theories to be endless, so too is the motion introduced into society by a regime that seeks politically to embody such a (mythical) struggle. The stability of the web of relationships and social and political structures that inform and shape the lives of individuals living together in a community is thereby destroyed. By calling on the axioms of the Idea that governs history, new classes of "objective" enemies can be invented *ad infinitum,* so that totalitarian terror can also be extended indefinitely. As Koestler showed, the ideas of "social class" and "class struggle" will serve this purpose in parallel ways.

Race- and class-ideas are not unique in their totalitarian possibilities, nor, if they are tempered in a given polity by other political ideas, do they necessarily lead to totalitarian excesses. Nevertheless, they pose a danger to the justice of any polity, as does the logic of any idea if it is made exclusive and absolute for the truth of human existence. The totality of human existence cannot be expressed by one idea, and certainly cannot be understood by spinning out the logic of any one idea of existence; its essence remains fundamentally mysterious, even if nearly all of its elements are open, though not with absolute certainty and clarity, to discursive theoretical and narrative articulation.

Arendt observed that, apart from being rooted in human experience, ideologies are persuasive because they provide those who believe in them "access to history." [25] We have seen in Koestler's literary example that "an ideology differs from a simple opinion in that it claims to possess either the key to history, or the solution for all the 'riddles of the universe,' or the intimate knowledge of the hidden universal laws which are supposed to rule nature and man." Racism and classism are not the only possible ideologies that would serve this purpose and thereby potentially inform totalitarian regimes,

25. *Ibid.,* 332.

but for any number of reasons, they have won out.[26] Consequently, these two ideologies are the most important to understand if we seek to understand a significant portion of the politics of modernity.

CONCLUSION

The words "National Socialist" never appear in Voegelin's two books on race-ideas. Sebba tells us that Voegelin could not "bring himself to use the [phrase]."[27] National socialism, however, was the vulgar descendant of the race theories he criticized and therefore the ultimate object of his attack. Looking backward, the crudity of National Socialist race biology still offends and its proponents remain objects of study, not participants in a discussion. It is nevertheless important briefly to note their speech, for it is in this vulgar form that ideological race-ideas are presented to the many. We find here all of the problematic components of race theory that we have analyzed.

By means of a "general folkish world conception," National Socialists form "a political creed which, in turn, by the strict organizational integration of large human masses thus made possible [by the creed], creates the precondition for the victorious struggle of this world view." The core idea of this "folkish concept" is that "the importance of mankind [is] in its basic racial elements." The ideology of the folkish concept "corresponds to the innermost will of Nature, since it restores that free play of forces which must lead to a continuous mutual higher breeding, until at last the best of humanity, having achieved possession of this earth, will have a free path for activity in domains which will lie partly above it and partly outside it." The freedom of the "best of humanity" can be justified not only as an end in itself, but for its prospective utility. In the future, "humanity must be faced by problems which only a highest race, become master people and supported by the means and possibilities of an entire globe, will be equipped to overcome."[28]

In this conception, the state, including its institutions, political apparatus, and functionaries, is a necessary means to an end. The end of the state in general is the "preservation of the racial existence

26. *Ibid.*, 159.
27. Sebba, "Prelude and Variations," 11.
28. Adolf Hitler, *Mein Kampf,* trans. Ralph Mannheim (Boston, 1971), 383, 384.

of man." For each individual race, the state is the political vessel of the race, and the race is the state's content. By means of the verbal and conceptual sleight-of-hand with which we are now familiar, race is asserted here to have the same empirical biological status as subspecies.[29] It can be bred and manipulated accordingly. The immediate end that the state serves and the means used to that end depend upon the character of the particular race for which it is the vessel. In every case, "the forces which create culture and values are based essentially on racial elements," hence the state's "highest task [is] the preservation and intensification of the race." "This preservation itself comprises first of all excellence as a race and thereby permits the free development of all the forces necessary in this race." Accordingly, the "highest purpose" of the National Socialist state is to preserve "those original racial elements which bestow culture and create the beauty and dignity of a higher mankind." This purpose is fulfilled most directly by sustaining by whatever means necessary the purity of the German race, which is, or is soon to become, the "higher mankind."[30]

The task of the administrators of the National Socialist racial state, therefore, is to ensure the vitality and integrity of the ascendant race. They are to preserve the race from "political, ethical, and moral contamination," and to prevent the "poisoning of the health of the national body."[31] Both forms of harm can result from the struggle of the world's races in history for ascendancy. But the members of the German race are intended by nature and history to be masters. The policies of the National Socialist state must be directed toward that end. How National Socialist policies of killing emerge from this ideology is made clear by the recorded statements of a high-ranking SS officer. The new "Führer class" is the racially predominant elite that is to be the "finest flower" emerging from the National Socialist program of purifying the race and making it great. This elite is selected and bred "in a negative sense by the ex-

29. *Ibid.*, 391, 385, 400–401.
30. *Ibid.*, 394, 393, 399ff. Further details of National Socialist "political biology" and its relationship to racial policy may be found in Helmuth Krausnick, "The Persecution of the Jews," trans. Dorothy Long, in Helmuth Krausnick, Hans Buchheim, Martin Broszat, and Hans-Adolf Jacobsen, *Anatomy of the SS State* (London, 1968), 14–19.
31. Hitler, *Mein Kampf,* 246.

149

termination of all racially and biologically inferior elements and by the radical removal of all incorrigible political opposition that refuses on principle to acknowledge the philosophical [sic] basis of the National Socialist State and its essential institutions."[32] From this basis, immersed in racist ideology, emerge the numerous genocidal initiatives, operations, and organizations of the Third Reich.

We should note two elements of this description. First, it depends for its persuasiveness on a prior claim about racial relationships in history, a claim whose problematic characteristics have been the subject of this essay. We have scanned briefly the central elements of this ideological assertion as it is crudely sketched out in Hitler's manifesto. Voegelin's analysis stripped all such racist accounts of their validity on philosophical and natural-scientific grounds. Second, "racially and biologically inferior elements" and "incorrigible political opposition" can in principle be endlessly defined, refined, and enlarged. Hence the possibility of endless terror and its attendant endless totalitarian motion. The essence of the ideological blueprint for totalitarian murder is provided in the statements of this officer of the *Schutz-Staffel*. The further totalitarian characteristics of both the ideological account of the role of the German race in history and of the public policy that results are clear from the preceding analysis.

The description of the development of the race-idea and its attendant philosophical difficulties is complete. The characteristics of the idea's form and content that lend it to ideological use are clear. The use of the race-idea as an explanation for the mystery of the historical process, its concomitant ideas of biological progress and continual forward motion that have their origin in biological doctrines of organic evolution, are the necessary ingredients for a totalitarian ideology. An exclusion of other, nonracial experiences and a further exclusion of questions, either through ignorance or willful malice, enable the race-idea to become the sole and guiding idea of a community. Its roots in experiences of the body and its claims for support in natural science give it an emotional persuasiveness that permits its initial takeover and denial of all other formative ideas of

32. Eugen Kogon, *The Theory and Practice of Hell,* trans. Heinz Norden (New York, 1949), 15.

150

a community, and that permit its adherents to make "scientific" deductions from its premise (racial differences and conflicts are inevitable and the moving force in history) that can become both the key to history and the policy statements of a totalitarian regime.[33] It should also be clear that race-ideas do not of necessity become race ideologies, but may take numerous forms depending on the configurations of other experiences and symbolizations of those experiences and on the other ideas that inform a particular society. Only certain kinds of people, having had particular kinds of experiences and being informed by particular configurations of ideas, believe there can be a key to unlock the meaning of history. They are those who are dissatisfied, for whatever reason, with their place in the mystery of social and historical existence.[34] An immanentist scientistic discourse becomes their key.

The race-idea in its vulgar form is antihistorical in two ways. First, it ends history because it has "solved" history. History solved is history finished, for if history is a story of the search for excellence, an unfolding of man's personal and collective nature, or a string of stories of great deeds and words, then its solution and its dissolution are equivalent. One does not search for an answer, or

33. "The tremendous power of persuasion inherent in the main ideologies of our times is not accidental. Persuasion is not possible without appeal to either experiences or desires, in other words to immediate political needs. Plausibility in these matters comes neither from scientific facts, as the various brands of Darwinists would like us to believe, nor from historical laws, as the historians pretend, in their efforts to discover laws according to which civilizations rise and fall. Every full-fledged ideology has been created, continued and improved as a political weapon and not as a theoretical doctrine. It is true that sometimes—and such is the case with racism—an ideology has changed its original political sense, but without immediate contact with political life none of them could be imagined. Their scientific aspect is secondary and arises first from the desire to provide water-tight arguments, and second because their persuasive power also got hold of scientists, who no longer were interested in the result of their research but left their laboratories and hurried off to preach to the multitude their new interpretations of life and world" (Arendt, *Totalitarianism*, 159).

34. Here we may refer to Arendt's *The Origins of Totalitarianism* as a whole. The development of dissatisfied masses of worldless people, searching for a place to belong, has a long history. It is these masses, and their leaders, members of what Arendt called the mob, who search for meaning in the processes of history. *The Origins of Totalitarianism* is an account of the genesis of the groups involved, and their gradual ascent to power.

151

better, a meaning, that has been revealed. If history is an immanent unfolding of immanent (biological) forces that may be described in terms of laws of process, then there is nothing left to do, except to conform to the fateful laws of the immanent process. Second, on the narrower level of human action, one belongs to one race having specifiable qualities, or one belongs to another. In any case, the fatefulness of one's genetic endowments determines the course of one's life, so that one not only must conform to the process of history, but accept that, within that process, there "is nothing much to do" (*RI*, 21). In Carus' immanentist theory of race, the demonic individual was called upon to express the fullness of his intellect and spirit within the possibilities of his physical form and his racial character. In the vulgar form of race ideology, this meaning for life is taken away, and we are left with what Voegelin called the "Averroistic moment" of the totalitarian regime: the exclusionary idea of the race permeates the mass uniformly, all equally participate in it, and all equally partake of the benefits of their participation. The idea is "total"; all meaning for individual and group is found in the membership of race.[35] All other ideas that might inform and differentiate the community have been eliminated, and a single idea permeates the intellectual and spiritual life (to use the terms somewhat loosely) of the mass. This mass can then be brought into motion in accordance with the laws of continual process, implied by a biological conception of the community and ideologically discovered in history itself.[36] Being entirely determines consciousness; the state has become the ahistorical articulation of immanent biological forces (*RI*, 22).

Voegelin's arguments concerning archetypes, ideas, symbols, and experience tell us that every rational discourse implies inherent laws, limits, and boundaries, within which speaking, acting, and even imagining take place. Action does not occur in a boundless space, but within the confines of a symbolic and iconic tradition; a particular act may be seen as a transgression of the boundaries of the tradition, or an expansion of its boundaries, or an activity within the boundaries. Thus, all actions are delimited and constrained by the logic of the boundaries. By "logic of the boundaries," I mean that every image and idea, in Voegelin's sense of the words, bears within

35. Voegelin, *Autoritäre Staat*, 23–24.
36. See Arendt, *Totalitarianism*, 464.

itself an interpretation of reality that implies its own, specific structure and order. The laws of the order determine the possibilities of speech, action, and often even of thought.

The structure of reality, defined by the boundaries, is not only immanent to a particular discourse; in a wider sense, there is also an absolute structure. The nature and form of the absolute structure is the intended object of theoretical discussion, and more importantly, the context of all human speech and action. The logic of the absolute boundaries is the context within which we may understand the various archetypes of reality, the images and symbols derived from them, and the possibilities of human activity. Voegelin argued that philosophical discussion could become trapped in the smaller, archetypical worlds of discourse; he himself attempted in every possible way to transcend particular archetypes in his own theoretical writings. Insofar as it is possible, the absolute limits of knowledge and experience must be explored and articulated by the political philosopher in order to come to terms with the meaning and implications of particular ideas.[37]

Ideological speculation, of which the poorer race theories may be considered an initial example, is an attempt to transgress the boundaries of understanding and experience, and to penetrate to the mystery of being. But because there are limits, because the membrane of symbol and experience is impermeable, ideological or philosophically impoverished speculations lead to a shrinking of human existence rather than an expansion. An "explanation" of existence in terms of a single idea is an occlusion of reality, not an explanation. We saw this in the several examples of attempts at explaining mysteries of existence that eclipsed not only the mystery itself, but also one or more of its constituent parts. It remains the task of the political philosopher to explore the elements of this mystery without destroying the integrity of human existence in its mysteriousness.

37. The boundaries of experience and knowledge were later articulated to greater theoretical depth by Voegelin in his symbol of the quaternarian structure of human existence. See *OH* I, 11ff.

Selected Bibliography

Arendt, Hannah. *The Human Condition*. Chicago, 1958.
————. *The Origins of Totalitarianism*. New York, 1973.
Bergson, Henri. *The Two Sources of Morality and Religion*. Translated by R. Ashly Audra and Cloudesly Brereton. Garden City, N.Y., 1935.
Bodenheimer, F. S. *The History of Biology: An Introduction*. London, 1958.
Breasted, James Henry. *A History of Egypt*. New York, 1912.
Burrowes, Robert. "Totalitarianism: The Revised Standard Version." *World Politics*, XXI (1968), 272–94.
Bueno, Anibal A. "Consciousness, Time and Transcendence in Eric Voegelin's Philosophy." In *The Philosophy of Order*, edited by Peter J. Opitz and Gregor Sebba. Stuttgart, 1981.
Coleman, William. *Biology in the Nineteenth Century: Problems of Form, Function, and Transformation*. New York, 1971.
Cooper, Barry. *The End of History: An Essay on Modern Hegelianism*. Toronto, 1984.
Darwin, Charles. *On the Origin of Species by Means of Natural Selection*. New York, 1951.
Friedrich, Carl J., and Zbigniew Brzezinski. *Totalitarian Dictatorship and Autocracy*. Cambridge, Mass., 1965.
Gardiner, Sir Alan. *Egypt of the Pharaohs*. Oxford, 1961.
Gasking, Elizabeth G. *Investigations into Generation, 1651–1828*. Baltimore, 1967.
Gobineau, Arthur de. *The Inequality of the Human Races*. Translated by Adrian Collins. New York, 1967.
Goldberg, Michael. *Jews and Christians: Getting Our Stories Straight*. Nashville, 1985.
————. *Theology and Narrative: A Critical Introduction*. Nashville, 1982.

155

Gollwitzer, Hellmut. . . . *und führen, wohin du nicht willst.* Munich, 1953.

Grube, G. M. A. *Plato's Thought.* Boston, 1958.

Halverson, William H. *A Concise Introduction to Philosophy.* New York, 1976.

Hanson, Norwood Russell. *Patterns of Discovery: An Inquiry into the Conceptual Foundations of Science.* Cambridge, Eng., 1958.

Harris, Kenneth A. "The Political Meaning of Death: An Existential Overview." *Omega,* II (1971), 227–39.

Harvey, William. "On Animal Generation." In *The Works of William Harvey,* translated and edited by R. Willis. London, 1847.

Hauerwas, Stanley. *The Peaceable Kingdom.* Notre Dame, Ind., 1983.

Havard, William C., Jr. "The Changing Pattern of Voegelin's Conception of History and Consciousness." *Southern Review,* VII (1971), 49–67.

———. "Notes on Voegelin's Contributions to Political Theory." In *Eric Voegelin's Thought: A Critical Appraisal,* edited by Ellis Sandoz. Durham, N.C., 1982.

Hodgson, Sandworth Hollway. *The Metaphysic of Experience.* Vol. II of 4 vols. London, 1898.

Jonas, Hans. *The Phenomenon of Life: Toward a Philosophical Biology.* Chicago, 1966.

Kant, Immanuel. *Critique of Practical Reason.* Translated by Lewis White Beck. New York, 1985.

Keil, C. F., and F. Delitzsche. *The Pentateuch.* Grand Rapids, 1981. Vol. I of Keil and Delitzsche, *Commentary on the Old Testament.* 10 vols.

Koestler, Arthur. *Darkness at Noon.* New York, 1941.

Kogon, Eugen. *The Theory and Practice of Hell.* Translated by Heinz Norden. New York, 1949.

Krausnick, Helmuth. "The Persecution of the Jews." Translated by Dorothy Long. In *Anatomy of the SS State,* by Helmuth Krausnick, Hans Buchheim, Martin Broszat, and Hans-Adolf Jacobsen. London, 1968.

Kuhn, Thomas. *The Structure of Scientific Revolutions.* Chicago, 1962.

Lifton, Robert Jay. *The Broken Connection.* New York, 1979.

Lifton, Robert Jay, and Eric Olson. *Living and Dying.* New York, 1974.

Mann, Thomas. *Joseph und seine Brüder.* Frankfurt am Main, 1960. Vol. VI of Mann, *Gesammelte Werke.* 13 vols.

Masterman, Margeret. "The Nature of a Paradigm." In *Criticism and the Growth of Knowledge,* edited by Imre Lakatos and Alan Musgrave. Proceedings of the International Colloquium in the Philosophy of Science, London, 1965, vol. 4. Cambridge, Eng., 1970.

Neumann, Sigmund. *Permanent Revolution: The Total State in a World at War.* London, 1942.

Nordenskiold, Erik. *The History of Biology.* London, 1929.

Polanyi, Michael. "The Republic of Science: Its Political and Economic Theory." *Minerva,* I (Autumn, 1962), 54–73.

Pritchard, James B., ed. *Ancient Near Eastern Texts Relating to the Old Testament.* Princeton, 1955.

Randall, John Herman, Jr. *Plato: Dramatist of the Life of Reason.* New York, 1970.

Reid, R. W. *Tongues of Conscience: War and the Scientists' Dilemma.* London, 1970.

Rosen, Stanley. "Ideas." *Review of Metaphysics,* XVI (1963), 407–41.

Russell, Bertrand. *The Problems of Philosophy.* Oxford, 1912.

Sandoz, Ellis, ed. *Eric Voegelin's Thought: A Critical Appraisal.* Durham, N.C., 1982.

———. *The Voegelinian Revolution: A Biographical Introduction.* Baton Rouge, 1981.

Schelling, Friedrich W. J. *Einleitung in die Philosophie der Mythologie.* Munich, 1928.

Sebba, Gregor. "Prelude and Variations on the Theme of Eric Voegelin." In *Eric Voegelin's Thought: A Critical Appraisal,* edited by Ellis Sandoz. Durham, N.C., 1982.

Singer, Charles. *A History of Biology.* New York, 1950.

Voegelin, Eric. *Der Autoritäre Staat.* Vienna, 1936.

———. *The Ecumenic Age.* Baton Rouge, 1974. Vol. IV of *Order and History.* 5 vols.

———. "The Growth of the Race Idea." *Review of Politics,* II (1940), 283–317.

———. "Industrial Society in Search of Reason." In *World Technology and Human Destiny,* edited by R. Aron. Ann Arbor, 1963.

———. *Israel and Revelation.* Baton Rouge, 1956. Vol. I of *Order and History.* 5 vols.

———. "The Mongol Orders of Submission to European Powers, 1245–1255." *Byzantion,* XI (1941), 378–413.

———. *The New Science of Politics: An Introduction.* Chicago, 1952.

———. "The Origins of Scientism." *Social Research,* XV (1948), 462–94.

———. *Rasse und Staat.* Tübingen, 1933.

———. *Die Rassenidee in der Geistesgeschichte von Ray bis Carus.* Tübingen, 1933.

———. Review of *The Origins of Totalitarianism,* by Hannah Arendt. *Review of Politics,* XV (1953), 68–85. With a reply by Hannah Arendt.

———. *Science, Politics, and Gnosticism.* Chicago, 1968.

157

————. *Über die Form des amerikanischen Geistes.* Tübingen, 1928.
————. *The World of the Polis.* Baton Rouge, 1957. Vol. II of *Order and History.* 5 vols.
Webb, Eugene. *Eric Voegelin: Philosopher of History.* Seattle, 1981.
Whitcomb, John C., and Henry B. Morris. *The Genesis Flood.* Philadelphia, 1961.
Yoder, John H. *The Priestly Kingdom.* Notre Dame, Ind., 1984.

Index

Abraham, 118
Angst, 126–29, 130
Archetypes: nature of, 12, 22; varieties
 of, 12–13; transformation of, 16,
 20–22, 83–85, 93, 94–97, 116,
 122–25, 127, 130, 141; and primal
 manner of seeing, 17–18; and philosophy, 19; and science, 19–20;
 and symbols, 20; embodiment of,
 23; efficacy of, 33; and narrative,
 133
Arendt, Hannah, 2, 137, 138, 139, 147,
 151 *n*33, *n*34
Amos of Tekoa, 1
Aesthetic community, 104
Aristotle, 35, 47
Asher (Israelite tribe), 117
Augustine, 101, 122

Baldwin, James Mark, 82
Beethoven, Ludwig van, 110
Benjamin (Israelite tribe), 117
Bergson, Henri, 2, 41
Blumenbach, Johann Friedrich, 91, 92
Bonaparte, Napoleon, 18
Brentano, Franz Clemens, 25, 27, 28
Bruno, Giordano, 65–66
Bueno, Anibal, 25
Buffon, Georges-Louis Leclerc, Count
 of, 84, 90, 91

Caesar, 18
Carus, Carl Gustav, 105, 112–13, 152
Christianity: and narrative, 120–21;
 early, 121; and body-ideas, 122–24
Claudias, Matthias, 6
Clauss, Ludwig, 113–14
Consciousness: theories of, 25–28;
 Voegelin's theory of, 28–30, 32

Dan (Israelite tribe), 117
Dante Alighieri, 110
Darwin, Charles Robert: theory of ori-
 gin of species, 67–69, 70–76
Death, 37, 98–100, 126–29
Demonic man, 103, 104, 113
Descartes, René, 35, 41, 46, 47, 88
Dualism, 39, 40–41, 46–47, 62, 90,
 112

Egypt, ancient: 23, 117, 119; cos-
 mology of, 13–14; political break-
 down of, 14–15
Einstein, Albert, 139–40
Enlightenment, 23
Epigenesis, 88, 90

Fate: 111; in race theory, 135
Fichte, Johann Gottlieb, 35
Fischer, Eugen, 81

159